AUTISM IN LOCKDOWN

Expert Tips and Insights on Coping with the COVID-19 Pandemic

FUTURE HORIZONS INC.

AUTISM IN LOCKDOWN

All marketing and publishing rights guaranteed to and reserved by:

FUTURE HORIZONS INC.

(800) 489-0727
(817) 277-0727
(817) 277-2270 (fax)
E-mail: info@fhautism.com
www.fhautism.com

ISBN: 978-1949177534

CONTENTS

CONTENTS

INTRODUCTION

This book would, quite simply, not exist without the Future Horizons and Sensory World authors who made it happen. I want to thank everyone for their swift and generous contributions. On April 25, I asked if any authors were interested in contributing to a little book about the quarantine, and the response was overwhelming. I don't say that lightly. The flood of response to my inbox literally brought tears to my eyes. Everyone wanted to help. We have the best authors in the world.

As you can imagine with such a project, time was of the essence. This book is one that is needed NOW, not next year (hopefully). The nine to twelve months we usually spend bringing a book from manuscript to final version had to be completed in just a few weeks.

To speed things along and get the needed information into your hands more quickly, we had to forgo the weeks of copyediting that usually go into a book. So please forgive any minor errors you may come across. You won't find perfection, but you will find information that is both insightful and helpful.

Also, the articles may have some overlap. We did not have the time for each author to see the final product and make minor adjustments. If you see that several authors mention a subject in their writings, this just means that issue is even more important.

This is the first book we made, knowing it would soon be obsolete. Soon enough we will not need this book, but you can keep it on your shelf as a collector's item.

Thank you so much and I hope this information helps you and your family during the quarantine months. Hang in there, everyone.

Jennifer Gilpin Yacio
President
Future Horizons

PART 1

COPING

COVID-19 AND AUTISM

Dr. Tony Attwood

t is important to remember that kids with autism have an acute sensitivity to anxiety in others. Anxiety is contagious.

There are so many reasons to be anxious all around us these days. We have news reports that discuss the 'killer' virus, along with a number of people who have died. And this number is rising, yet to reach the peak. Yet another reason to be worried!

Kids with autism are feeling the pain of the world. They see scenes on television and have such empathy, that they have trouble moving on from what they have seen.

They are likely to develop anxiety for the health of their parents and/or grandparents. Add to that the fear of uncertainty. We are in uncertain times. This is challenging for all of us, but more so for people with autism, who rely on routine so strongly.

So, what do we do? Family and caregivers must be calm, confident and optimistic, so their kids can pick up on this attitude. If fear is contagious, so is calm.

One way to keep a sense of calm in your household is to limit your news time. Watch the news once a day, not continuous 24-hour news cycle. Then turn it off and go play a game or take a walk. Discuss what you have seen and what gives you hope. Help them digest what they have just seen.

INCREASE IN THE SIGNS OF AUTISM

Many of the characteristics of autism are coping mechanisms or associated with anxiety and stress. So, when stress levels go up, so do the signs of autism.

You may very well see an increase in social withdrawal, routines and rituals, sensory sensitivity, and engagement in their special interest.

MANAGING INTENSE ANXIETY

So, what do we do to take care of the anxiety causing the rise in autistic behaviour? As we discussed earlier, family and caregivers need to remain calm.

First off, validate their feelings. You can say something like, "I can see that you are feeling worried about the future, and that is understandable".

Please, do not ask the person to explain what they are anxious about. This may cause even more anxiety and you may see a lack of eloquence, coherence and sequence in their attempt to explain. What you need to do is move through and out of the distress, not return to where it began.

If the person is unreasonable at this stage, then reason will be ineffective. Empathize and explain that the intense anxiety or distress will go away.

Praise and encourage them as they become calmer and share gratitude that the anxiety is going away.

Validate and sit with feelings as they decompress. Help them notice feelings in their body, then use a strategy to help reach a calmer state of mind (e.g. grounding, breathing, act in line with values and goals etc).

INFORMATION

Sharing information during a crisis is necessary. Yet how do we do this without causing more distress? Try to share the information you have in an honest, reassuring and practical way.

Model how to cope with the information they are receiving. Do this by vocalizing your thoughts. This helps encourage positive self-talk.

Health is on everyone's mind and the inherent difficulty of perceiving low-level signs of infection and pain are an aspect of autism that is relevant in determining if the kid is coming down with the virus. Use a thermometer for objective information. If they do not show a fever, this may help calm anxieties.

CHANGES IN DAILY ROUTINE

Everyone's routines are disrupted, and new routines are taking their place. It is important to help people with autism cope with change as much as possible.

Suddenly everything is on hold. It is like a holiday, but we are unable to do what you like to do on a holiday. This is very frustrating.

We are not having family gatherings and outings anymore and cannot see the people we may want to see. This is even more frustrating and sometimes anxiety producing. What if something happens to our loved ones while we are away from them? This uncertainty is tough for all of us to deal with, but we know our loved ones are also being safe in their homes. Explain that and explain what makes you feel safe about your loved ones who are away from you. Spend some quality time with people you are worried about on a video chat.

We all have so much more free time and it is important that this time is not totally taken up by the computer. DO get outside if you can. A walk can do wonders for your mind. Also important is having a 'to do' list of things you can complete around the house to get rid of the anxiety energy you now have. Some of the best activities are those that bring order out of chaos, such as decluttering the attic or basement. Organize your closet and get rid of old clothes. When you create order out of chaos, you gain a sense of control in an uncontrolled world. This is necessary for our collective sanity right now.

STRATEGIES TO MANAGE STRESS

There is often conflict in the family due to being cooped up together. It is easy to take up your frustrations on the ones you are stuck with but try to use some anger management and step away when you find yourself losing your sense of calm.

As much as you can, maintain a routine and make sure to include exercise and yoga/meditation. If you have therapy, continue this therapy via Zoom or Skype. Most therapists are still available for you.

Do a quick medication review. Do any dosages need to change? Talk to your medical doctor.

On the plus side (and there is always a plus side), life is now more autism friendly. There are no touching and hugs on greeting and no crowds. How lovely!

And let's end on the important note that vaccines are being developed by scientists, *many of whom have autism.* We need scientists with autism to end the pandemic. People who are very much like you are needed now more than ever. ∎

 **DR. TONY ATTWOOD** is a practicing clinical psychologist with more than 25 years of experience. He has worked with over 2,000 individuals of all ages with Asperger's syndrome. He presents workshops and runs training courses for parents, professionals, and individuals with AS all over the world, and is a prolific author of articles and books on the subject. He is the author of multiple books, including the *Exploring Feelings* series, *The Complete Guide to Asperger's Syndrome*, and the co-author of *Autism and Girls: World-Renowned Experts Join Those with Autism Syndrome to Resolve Issues That Girls and Women Face Every Day!*

CAROL'S CLUB
PANDEMIC STORIES

Carol Gray

I receive many requests for Social Stories™ on a variety of topics. Some of the most difficult topics are related to catastrophes, shootings, natural disasters, and most recently, the COVID-19 pandemic. Initially these topics can seem to defy description or explanation and hold me hostage to an uncomfortable writer's block. What's interesting about Social Stories™, though, is that the defined format rescues me every time. It focuses my thoughts and creates an unexpected "angle" or route through a difficult topic that wasn't part of my original plan. These "discovered" Stories seem to have something for everyone, of any age, and enjoy instant popularity as they are released.

This was the case with "Third Grade Isn't a Place" and "Watching a Pandemic on Television." I began writing each of them with a clear outline in mind, only to have them dissolve in favor of unexpected Stories that seemed to write themselves.

Stay Safe and Take Care,

Carol Gray

WATCHING A PANDEMIC ON TELEVISION

A pandemic is when many people in a large area become sick with the same illness. A new virus called COVID-19 has caused a worldwide pandemic. Each day there is news about the pandemic. People watch television for information. It's helpful to understand what I see and hear.

Many children find that it is easier to learn about a pandemic with an adult. Adults have lived a long time. They have seen many serious reports on television and can answer questions. Talking with adults helps many children feel less confused and more comfortable again.

Reporters go to communities and hospitals to talk with experts. They talk to people about the pandemic and take videos and photos to show on television. What I see on television may not be happening now.

Other times, a newscast may be "live." When this happens, what I see on television is happening at the same time someplace else.

Many newer televisions have a big, sharp picture screen. This makes it fun to watch my shows because it feels so *realistic*, like I am really there. When news about a pandemic is on television, it's helpful to remember that I am *not*

there. Only the television is in my home, not the COVID-19 virus or the pandemic.

During a pandemic, my family may be home for a while. We may have new routines. Some routines will be about the same as before the pandemic. For example, if we usually have dinner at about 6 o'clock, and it's almost 6 o'clock now, we'll probably be having dinner soon. In fact, many other families will also be having dinner soon.

During a pandemic, children and adults may feel worried or concerned. They know that many people are very sick. It's safe and okay to feel uncomfortable for a while. Adults can help.

Very young children may be quite happy. They may not be worried or confused. This is okay. They are too young to understand about pandemics.

A very big pandemic will be on television for many days. The same video or story may be on tv many times. This may make it seem like a sad event is happening over and over, even though it happened once.

During a pandemic, people on television may use confusing words or phrases. For example, someone may say that our country is "at war," even though our country is not fighting with another country. In this case, "at war" means that the pandemic is a problem for everyone, and we are working hard to end it. Parents can help if I am confused by words or phrases that I hear on television.

As I grow, knowing about serious events on television may make it easier for me to understand what I am seeing, and to know what to do. It's safe to feel confused, sad, or concerned, and to ask questions. Many people feel that way about pandemics. There may be things we can all do to help.

THIRD GRADE ISN'T A PLACE. THIS IS OKAY.

I am a third grader in Miss Scott's classroom at Lincoln School. Avs long as I am in third grade, I am a third grader, even when I am *not* in Miss Scott's classroom,

too! That's because third grade isn't a place.

This school year, I am a third grader wherever I go. I am in third grade at school, home, and the grocery store; and on Saturdays, Sundays, and during the holidays, too!

Being a third grader means that I am part of a group of kids who are about the same age and learning similar things.

We started third grade in a classroom. Miss Scott gave us assignments to practice new skills.

She checked our work to be sure that we understood.

Now there is a pandemic. Pandemics happen once in a very long while. A pandemic is when many people in a large area become sick. COVID-19 is a virus that is moving around the world from one person to another.

This past March, people began staying home from school and work to stay safe from COVID-19 and keep it from spreading. Lincoln School closed to keep students healthy. It took adults a few weeks to decide the best place for children to finish their school year.

Adults have decided the safest place for children to finish their school year is at home. Miss Scott's classroom is closed. This is okay. Third grade is open.

Working at home is another way to finish being a third grader.

Just like before the pandemic, Miss Scott gives us assignments to practice new skills, and checks our work to be sure that we understand.

Our moms, dads, grandparents, or older brothers or sisters may help, too. When they were younger, they learned the skills that we are learning now. They may know how to help if we are confused or stuck.

Miss Scott is teaching us all that we need to know to finish third grade. That way, we'll be ready to start fourth grade. ■

CAROL GRAY is the author of *The New Social Story*™ *Book*. She has over twenty-five years of experience educating students with autism. Carol initiated the use of Social Stories™ in 1991 and has written numerous articles, chapters, and books on the subject. Currently, Carol works privately with students, parents, and professionals in a variety of educational and vocational settings. Every year, Carol gives many presentations and workshops throughout the world. She addresses topics related to the teaching of social understanding, bullying prevention, and friendship skills. Carol has received several awards for her work and international contributions to the education of individuals with autism and those who work on their behalf. She lives in Grand Rapids, Michigan.

DEALING WITH THE
NEW NORMAL

Jed Baker, PhD

WHAT DO I TELL MY KIDS ABOUT COVID-19?

Tell your kids what they need and want to know, but no need to introduce traumatizing stories of those struggling to breathe or dying separated from their family. Here's what you can say:

FOR VERBAL KIDS: Explain that there is a virus that is very tiny you cannot see it. It is very contagious, which means it's easy for one person to give it to another when they are near each other. If people breathe it into their bodies through their nose or mouth or get it in their eyes, it can make people sick. Most people will not get sick from it; but some may have a fever, cough and some shortness of breath for a week or two. A few people, especially the elderly, can get very sick and need to go to the hospital.

To protect yourself from getting it or spreading it to others, we must stay at least 6 feet or more from others and wear a mask in public areas to cover our mouths and noses. If no one has the virus in your family you do not have to stay away from family members. If you touch things in public or packages delivered to your house, wash your hands afterwards before touching your face.

FOR LESS VERBAL KIDS: Use the following link from Autism Society of America to find a good picture story that explain these same ideas through a comic book like sequence: *https://theautismeducator.ie/wp-content/uploads/2020/03/The-Corona-Virus-Free-Printable-Updated-2-The-*

Autism-Educator-.pdf?fbclid=IwAR0R3o7TJSgqoZ3_0aEZnFDt8X0qVfszz-3Bu8izIbuQT3n8RxqI7U5SHcQg. The picture sequence can serve as a start to show how the virus can make people sick, the need to wash your hands, and how some places are closed. Industrious parents may want to use the format to make their own picture books with pictures of their family and places they used to go.

WHAT IF MY CHILDREN ARE WORRIED THEY OR FAMILY MEMBERS WILL GET VERY SICK?

As I describe in my book, *Overcoming Anxiety in Children and Teens* (Baker 2015), there are several ways to rein in out-of-control anxiety.

For verbal kids, try getting them to "Think Like a Scientist." Scientist use scientific evidence and reasoning to help guide their beliefs. When individuals have run away fears, we always ask two questions to help them think like a scientist:

1. Are you overestimating the probability of something bad happening? Fearful thought: "I will get COVID and get very sick!" Let's look at the evidence. Most individuals are at very low risk of becoming ill. Both because they can lower the risk of getting the virus and because they are unlikely to get gravely ill from it. There are many things we can do to dramatically lower the probability of getting COVID-19. Social distancing, hand hygiene, not touching your face, and wearing protective gear like masks all limit the possibility of getting the virus.

2. Are you overestimating the severity of illness from COVID-19? Fearful thought: "If I get it I will die." Let's look at the evidence. Though there is no doubt COVID-19 can kill some individuals, the vast majority of people have mild or no illness. According to epidemiologists, the death rate may be as low as .5 to 1 percent when *all* the true positive cases are counted. Fatality risk rises for those who are sick enough to need hospital support, but most still survive. That means over 99 percent of people survive.

Thinking like a scientist neither grossly underestimates nor overestimates the risks. The risk to a population is high (1 percent is a lot of people), yet the odds for any individual dying are still extremely low.

WAYS TO TURN DOWN THE VOLUME OF ANXIETY. Besides "thinking like a scientist" there are ways to help reduce the intensity of anxious feelings. We know that sustained exercise that increases heart rate for 30 minutes or more greatly reduces anxiety for hours after the activity. In addition, mindfulness meditation has also been shown to reduce anxiety. Both exercise and mindfulness have been shown to reduce anxiety as well as antidepressant/ antianxiety medicines in a handful of studies. I often use a free website, *www. fragrantheart.com*, for downloading brief audio meditation guides. For less verbal kids who may not understand the language of a meditation guide, relaxing spa like music has been shown to reduce anxiety. For example, just listening to the tune Weightless, by Marconi Union, was shown in a British study to reduce anxiety. Lastly antidepressant/anxiety medications can be a useful tool to reduce anxiety over short or longer periods of time. Though some of these medications are habit forming, many are not and can be used briefly to help folks get through a difficult period of time.

HOW DO I HELP MY KIDS ACCEPT THE NEW LIMITATIONS ON THEIR LIVES?

Although some kids with autism do not seem to mind having activities cancelled or staying close to home, most eventually grow frustrated with having to limit their interactions. One way to motivate compliance with staying away from friends or others is to invoke the notion that such social distancing is heroic. Kids who are willing to stay away from others insure that they and others will not get sick. They are literally saving lives. Ironically, by staying away from the people they miss, they are insuring those people will be around when the COVID-19 crisis is over.

We must also give our kids alternatives to the activities they miss. They can video chat with friends and teachers they miss, participate in hobbies like arts and crafts, cooking, music, dance and exercise. They can and should go outside as long as they maintain a distance from others. They can still order many of the foods they like and play the games they enjoy.

Parents may need a lot of patience with their kids as they slowly grieve the temporary loss of activities. A normal first stage of grief is denial, and kids may refuse to accept the limitations initially. As time goes by their protests may yield to sadness. Eventually though they may come to accept the new normal and embrace new activities to replace what was lost.

HOW DO I HELP MY KID CONTINUE TO LEARN FROM HOME?

As parents scramble to juggle their own work with caring round the clock for their kids and teaching their children at home, it becomes crucial to create some kind of schedule to help structure all this extra home time. Visual schedules can be created with the help of the visual scheduler app and samples of simple schedules for things like getting dressed can be found at the following link: *https://www.autismspeaks.org/sites/default/files/2018-08/Visual%20 Supports%20Tool%20Kit.pdf.* When setting up a schedule, keep in mind that parents do not need to recreate the amount of work attempted in school. For young children, and hour of instruction broken up through the day may be enough. For middle and high school students, several hours of classwork may be more appropriate. The schedule can be set up with less preferred tasks scheduled before a rewarding activity. For example, math followed by dance break, reading followed by game time, science followed by mealtime, etc.

In addition to using rewarding activities to motivate students to do less preferred work tasks, you can also make the work look less intimidating. Shorten the task by limiting the number of items or how long you will work and start with easy items the child can do before frustrating items. Kids are more likely to maintain motivation if they experience success with the work initially. Also, make school tasks more fun by turning desk work into hands-on activities. For example, math and science can become a cooking activity where one must measure out ingredients and halve or double recipes. Reading and writing activities can be set up where kids may have to read words that give clues as to where interesting things are hidden in the house, or write sentences requesting to play games so that the use of language leads to a fun activity.

One of the most important things to teach your children is that they are not supposed to know how to do their work immediately. We must combat the tendency for kids to think they are unintelligent if they do not understand something. We can do this by explaining, before they attempt to work, that they are not supposed to know it, and that people learn by trying, making mistakes and getting help. We can even reward them for trying it, making mistakes and asking for help, rather than rewarding them for correct work. In this way we reward the process of learning rather than the outcome.

Many of these ideas and more can be found in my books, *No More Meltdowns and Overcoming Anxiety in Children and Teens* available on my amazon author page: *https://www.amazon.com/Jed-Baker/e/B001JP01XG/ref=dp_byline_cont_book_1.* ■

 **JED BAKER, PhD** is the director of the Social Skills Training Project, an organization serving individuals with autism and social communication problems. He writes, lectures, and provides training internationally on the topic of social skills training and managing challenging behaviors. He is an award-winning author of 8 books, including *The Social Skills Picture Book; The Social Skills Picture Book for High School and Beyond; No More Meltdowns: Positive Strategies for Managing and Preventing Out-of-Control Behavior; No More Victims: Protecting those with Autism from Cyber Bullying, Internet Predators & Scams; Overcoming Anxiety in Children and Teens;* and *School Shadow Guidelines*. His work has also been featured on *ABC World News, Nightline*, the CBS *Early Show*, and the Discovery Health Channel.

TIPS FOR CONNECTING WITH AND SUPPORTING YOUR CHILD DURING LOCKDOWN

Dr. Roya Ostovar and Dr. Krista DiVittore

I f we know anything about kids with autism spectrum disorders, it is that transitions are difficult and require lots of planning and preparation on the parents' part. So much of parents' efforts, experiences, education and training focuses on preparing your child so they can respond effectively to change and experience transitions as seamlessly as possible. But how do you prepare your child for the unimaginable and for what you are struggling to understand yourself? That's what has happened with COVID-19 and the lockdown we are experiencing. Most schools were in session one day and they were not the following day. After-school programs, playgrounds, groups, pools and more closed almost overnight leaving us all in lockdown and at home all day.

Though supporting children full time and around the clock at home seemed daunting at first, once parents found their footing they realized that many of the skills they had learned throughout their child's life, with slight modifications, could easily translate to the current situation. The tips proposed here are just reminders of what most of you probably already know and have used in the past.

It is likely that with school, extra-curricular activities, and/or appointments prior to the lockdown your child was receiving support in multiple areas from multiple people. Parents are now required to tend to all the needs of the child. Any way that we look at these circumstances, we come to the same conclusion "this is hard." Parents, we know you are doing the best you can. We encourage you to take moments each day to take care of yourself, too. You are better able to be present and helpful for your child when you set aside some time to take a break, do something you enjoy, and/or make healthy choices for you, too. Give yourself time to rest, reflect, and rejuvenate.

We have the mindset that children with autism are doing their best every day. They are not trying to be uncooperative or difficult. They are not looking for a secondary gain or manipulation or pretending to have sensitivities to get special attention. Even if they don't outwardly show it, every child wants to do better. Their dysregulation often stems from discomfort, feeling unsettled or scared, anxiety or not understanding. In this time of uncertainty, we know that children across the country are doing their best to make sense of it all and we wanted to provide some support and tips for parents looking for some ideas and ways to connect and support their children during lockdown.

The following information is based on Dr. Roya Ostovar's and Dr. Krista DiVittore's combined experience working with individuals with autism and other neurodevelopmental disorders, and Dr. Roya Ostovar's book *The Ultimate Guide to Sensory Processing Disorder* (2009) and their book *5 Things You Need to Know About Social Skills Coaching* (2017).

CONNECTING WITH YOUR CHILD

There are many variations of how your child may respond to the changes in their routine. Children are experiencing daily, sometimes hourly challenges because of a change in their routine, unknown expectations, or confusion. Often, these challenges can be overwhelming and exhausting. This will affect parents and other family members in the home, who can often find it daunting to include their child in everyday activities, especially if those activities involve unpredictable events or environments that are potentially distressing for the child.

Almost everybody is experiencing an increased level of baseline stress at this time, including children. While most adults may be able to articulate their feelings and thoughts about their stress. Children may have more difficulty, and children within the autism spectrum often have even more difficulty. The latter subset of children often is living with neurodevelopmental differences that affect how they experience stress, such as higher or lower sensitivities to their environment, heightened or decreased awareness of their bodily functions, decreased intuitive ability to identify how they feel, etc. They often experience increased distress to transitions, unpredictability, and changes to their routine, all of which may lead to dysregulation. As parents know, their children will communicate distress by "shutting down" or "acting out" with little intuitive ability to communicate what they are feeling or why.

Connecting with them requires the parent to think through ways to increase the likelihood that their child will be able to engage in activities, including connecting with you and the rest of the family. As you have to put on even more hats than usual, including teacher, occupational therapist, social skills coach, etc., we want to encourage you to focus more on your connection with your child and prioritizing that alliance of trust and predictability with you. Here are some potentially helpful strategies to help decrease distress and increase the likelihood that your child will engage with you:

- **PLANNING.** Creating a weekly and daily schedule can be helpful for your child to transition to a new routine and learn new expectations. These strategies help with organization and structure, reducing unhelpful feelings of anticipation and stress for the child.

  - If each day or some days are similar, create a checklist that can be laminated for re-use or photocopy that you can quickly fill-in as needed.

  - Provide written and verbal schedules. Use priming and pre-teaching (exposing the child ahead of time what may arise later) to prepare for what is coming up.

  - Discuss expectations for the day and for each activity. Include them in planning each day's events, meal planning, etc. as much as you can.

  - Prepare the child in advance, as much as you can, for changes or transitions.

- **LISTEN TO YOUR CHILD.** Words are important, but perhaps even more important, is their behavior. Behavior is a form of communication and a change in behavior can provide very helpful information to identify increasing distress in your child. Instead of focusing on the behavior and what your child is doing or not doing, try to figure out what your child is trying to communicate to you through his or her behavior.

  - Your child will communicate in some way how they feel about what is occurring around them, with their words, behavior, mood, affect, nonverbal cues (facial expressions, gestures, body language). Being in tune with changes in their behavior can help parents manage expectations, identify potential sources of distress, and help the child re-regulate so they can re-engage.

  - Gauge how much activity or communication your child is up for having in the moment. Take your child's lead to determine what and how much they are up for. For example, if they are exhausted or needing movement/sensory stimulation, help them address those needs first.

  - If your child is showing that they are in a space to engage with you, let them know how proud of them you are in how they are adjusting to the newness, in how they are using their helpful regulation strategies, in the drawings that they have completed since being at home, etc. No accomplishment is too small. Children may not be intuitively motivated to regularly interact, so it is okay to put in the effort to make it a positive interaction for them. Make sure it is genuine!

  - Engage in preferred topics and interests. Have a conversation that they care about.

  - Ask your child how they feel. You may have to be specific in your questions and accept yes/no for answers. Are they having fun? Are they bored? Are they confused? Are they upset? What does it mean when they say "fine"? Your authentic curiosity will be helpful here and with this information, acknowledge and validate the feelings they express to you. Then ask follow-up questions to help your child troubleshoot and problem-solve anything distressing.

- Encourage your child to take a break when they are starting to feel frustrated, overwhelmed, or stressed throughout the day. You may also cue them to take a break, when you notice a change in behavior that could lead to further dysregulation.

- **ASK WHAT THE CHILD WANTS TO DO WITH PEOPLE IN THE HOME AND WHO THEY WANT TO CONNECT WITH OUTSIDE OF THE HOME.** It is important to help your child maintain connections with others during lockdown, especially adolescents who may feel increasingly self-conscious about being accepted by others.

  - Set up social opportunities within the home that incorporate your child's preferred interests, such as building something together, playing certain games, going for walks, etc. that will provide opportunities for positive connection with others.

  - Help your child identify people outside of the home that they would like to maintain a connection with, such as family members, friends from school, mentors, etc.

  - Collaboratively strategize on how to set up phone calls and/or video chats with these people, as well as topics to talk about/questions to ask. If they seem to be nervous about these calls, you can always roleplay or let them know that you can be there during the call for support. You can also help them decide on a time limit and practice how to end a conversation, if/when they need to.

- **DON'T PANIC!** If you see your child struggling, speak calmly to them and use language they are used to hearing. Now is not the time to use new techniques. If they are being safe toward themselves, others, and their environment, it is okay to give them space and let them know that you are outside of the door when they are ready for you and that you will check in with them in a few minutes.

- **USE HUMOR AND HAVE FUN.** It is no mystery that when used appropriately, laughter and humor can almost immediately lighten up the mood, relax a tense moment, and reduce stress, anxiety, and frustration. This is an amazingly helpful tool that can diffuse a potentially stressful or explosive situation rather quickly. In this case, humor works best when it is generalized or when you joke about yourself to make a point. For example, when you observe a child struggling to manipulate a pair of scissors, make a lighthearted comment about how it can be frustrating for anyone or how sometimes the same thing happens to you. Be genuine and treat the child in an age-/developmentally appropriate manner. Adolescents are especially sensitive to comments and treatment they consider "babyish," so be especially mindful of your tone of voice and the words you use with them.

- **GIVE SIMPLE, PRECISE DIRECTIONS, AND BREAK TASKS DOWN INTO SMALLER STEPS.** Make things more manageable. Ease any anticipated confusion by saying something like "I know this is a lot," or "this can be confusing," and offer an opportunity for questions to be asked. And let them know that you can provide support along the way as they need it.

ANSWERING TOUGH QUESTIONS

For some children, they have great difficulty integrating incoming information and experiences, making sense of them, and making accurate and helpful inferences. New experiences, changes in what they are used to, and ambiguity of future expectations can increase anxiety. Difficult questions may be asked. You might also start the conversation with your child to encourage asking any questions that may be lingering. It is okay if you don't know the answer or do not know how to initially answer a question. There is an abundant amount of information being thrown out there and sometimes it is hard to organize it for ourselves, nonetheless, answering the questions our children may ask us.

- Listen carefully to what your child is asking you, pause to fully understand what the underlying question may be, and determine what the most pertinent information is to the question. You must also, of course, take your child's age and developmental level (level of cognitive and psychosocial maturity) into consideration.

- Think about how things are being said, such as your tone of voice. Be logical, organized, concise, and concrete. Avoid jargon, double meanings, sarcasm, and teasing.

- Wait for your child to take the information in and respond. If you did not understand what it is they were asking, ask for more clarity. If you do not know, let them know that you will investigate it and get back to them. Then do it.

- Provide simple explanations of what is going on. Acknowledge that there are challenges and, as a result, changes to everybody's schedules and environments. Do not minimize the effect that it has on their life.

- Ask your child how they feel about what is going on and acknowledge their feelings. You may recognize an underlying feeling that they are not explicitly stating. You can acknowledge their feeling by saying something like, "It looks like all of these changes might overwhelm you" or "It sounds like you are a little nervous about what the future holds."

- If some dysregulation starts to occur, check your own response. The child is not acting out on purpose. The child is likely uncomfortable and/ or overwhelmed with the information that they are learning. Their internal experience of increased anxiety may be boiling over. It is probably best to continue to validate how overwhelming the situation is and their experience of it, as well as shifting to another topic or activity to disrupt the dysregulation and help them re-regulate with preferred topics or coping strategies.

- Reassure your child. Things are unpredictable. You will not know the answer to all of their questions. That is okay. Reassure your child that you will be figuring things out and you will help them get through whatever happens next.

CREATING A LOW STRESS/SENSORY-FRIENDLY DAYS

Home is often a place of safety and protection for the child that they come home from school to. With the changes for lockdown, there may be increased demands for parents to work and other siblings to be engaged in school, so the environment may have shifted. Especially if there are academic expectations for your child, it is important for them to have a space that they will best be able to engage in schoolwork. Ultimately, you are creating an environment that is less eventful.

- Within your house, set up a space that can be simplified, maybe a desk or table against a bare wall to decrease visual sensory overload. Ideally, a place that can be quiet and with less activity happening around them. Provide them with headphones if they have video classes to attend to decrease auditory distractions from others working in the home. Make sure the child's seat is stable, comfortable, and cushioned if needed. Since body awareness and the relationship of the body to space can be an area of weakness, this stability and comfort can help the child remain upright and focused on the task at hand. If they need fidgets or other tools to help them stay focused, set one or two options out for them to access.

- Sensory integration breaks are a key component to the day. Despite our old-fashioned ideas about attention, sitting quietly in the same position does not necessarily facilitate learning. In fact, many individuals, both children and adults, learn and work better and are more productive with some background noise or while moving. These are brief timeouts that a child can take as needed and/or on a scheduled basis to regroup, modulate, reorganize the senses, and regain the ability to return to the activity at hand. These breaks can occur through reminders from an adult or by the child's own initiative as a way to prevent problems, such as shutting down, meltdowns, overactivity, inattention, fidgeting, and other unproductive responses to sensory problems. Depending on the child's needs, sensory integration breaks could include a variety of activities, including movement activities or quiet space.

- Provide the option for the child to finish tasks in segments and allow extra time, as needed. Be clear about expectations, but flexible in the process. Let the child choose tasks and how to do them, if possible. ∎

DR. ROYA OSTOVAR is an Assistant Professor at Harvard Medical School in the Department of Psychiatry. She is a Clinical Neuropsychologist and the Director for the Center for Neurodevelopmental Services (CNS), a program serving those with Autism Spectrum Disorders, at McLean Hospital, the largest psychiatric affiliate of Harvard Medical School. An internationally recognized expert in the fields of Autism Spectrum Disorders, Non-Verbal Learning Disorder, Social Pragmatics Disorder, Social Skills Coaching, and Sensory Processing Disorder. Dr. Ostovar is the author of *The Ultimate Guide to Sensory Processing Disorder*, which received a *Creative Child Magazine*'s Preferred Choice Award, *5 Things You Need to Know About Social Skills Coaching*, and the *Autism Inventory of Development (AID™)*, both published by Future Horizons.

DR. KRISTA DIVITTORE is a clinical psychologist in private practice who works directly with adolescents and adults with a variety of mental health disorders, including neurodevelopmental disorders and psychiatric disorders. Her previous work includes staff clinical psychologist at the Center of Neurodevelopmental Services, a program serving those with Autism Spectrum Disorder at McLean Hospital, the psychiatric teaching hospital of Harvard Medical School where she was appointed an Instructor in the Department of Psychiatry. She uses various skills-based modalities including Cognitive Behavioral Therapy (CBT), Dialectical Behavior Therapy (DBT), and Acceptance and Commitment Therapy (ACT) to help individuals master skills that allow them to be more effective and fulfilled in their personal interpersonal lives. She is a coauthor for *5 Things You Need to Know About Social Skills Coaching*.

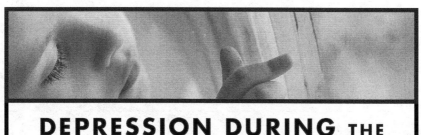

DEPRESSION DURING THE LOCKDOWN

Dr. Katherine Saint and Carlos Torres, BS

We are all at risk for depression during this time! We have all lost something. Freedom, activities, seeing friends, going to some of our favorite places. Our routines are different. Some of us are getting bored and restless! Some of us have lost ways we can be productive, and it is causing some self-esteem issues. The good news is there are things we can do to fight depression and we can turn this situation into something that has a really positive impact! So let's dive in!

DEPRESSION SYMPTOM CHECKLIST

In this section, we would like to work on self-awareness of problematic symptoms related to depression and autism spectrum disorder. To get better, we need to be aware of what we are feeling. Here is a self-assessment to reflect on symptoms of depression.

The following symptoms are commonly associated with depression. Describe what your experiences have been like with these symptoms. Identifying these symptoms will help us create a treatment plan for you! Answer based on how often you have experienced these symptoms in the last month.

1. Feelings of sadness/hopelessness/irritability most of the day.
   Describe for each emotion: _____

   _____

   _____

   What triggers these feelings? _____

   _____

   _____

   Is there a time of day that triggers this? _____

   _____

   _____

2. Decreased interest and/or enjoyment in activities you used to enjoy.
   Describe _____

   _____

   _____

3. Trouble sleeping and/or sleeping too much.
   Describe _____

   _____

   _____

4. Low energy and/or increased restlessness.
   Describe _____

   _____

   _____

5. Feelings of worthlessness/negative thoughts/excessive guilt, etc.
   Describe _____

   _____

   _____

6. Difficulty concentrating, focusing and completing or starting tasks.

Describe _____

_____

_____

7. Thoughts of suicide or self-harm.
   Describe _____

_____

_____

8. Struggling with the change in routine caused by COVID-19.
   Describe _____

_____

_____

9. Struggling with losses (activities, people, places etc.) caused by COVID-19
   Describe _____

_____

_____

10. Increased anger (yelling, throwing, breaking things etc.)
    Describe _____

_____

_____

If you are struggling with a lot of these points, it is ok, and you are not alone. The good news is there are things you can do that will help you reduce these symptoms.

INCREASING THE FEEL-GOOD CHEMICALS

This section is focusing on chemicals in your body that can fight depression. Dopamine is a chemical in your body that makes you feel good, and motivates you (Koob, 1996). Certain activities can help you produce dopamine. Use these questions to help figure out healthy ways you can add dopamine into your life.

1. Exercise produces dopamine. List below types of physical activities that you could do to help your body feel better.

_____

_____

_____

_____

2. Healthy relationships produce dopamine. List below behaviors you can do to help develop closer friendships. For example, who would you be willing to text, call or videochat. Maybe you have more ideas for ways you can connect with people right now. People are more available than normal right now because of so many places being closed.

_____

_____

_____

_____

3. Doing things that line up with your values produces dopamine. List below activities that you can do on a daily basis that take anywhere from 10 minutes to several hours that line up with your values. Examples could include reading books, spending time with family, or joining game groups.

_____

_____

_____

_____

4. When you notice that you are struggling, it is helpful to do two-minute value activities. Even two minutes of doing a value-based activity can give you dopamine. List here activities that are two minutes or less that relate to your values.

Example: If you value health and music you could do push-ups and listen to a song.

_____

_____

_____

_____

_____

Here is a list of 25 activities that you might try to fight depression! Write down the ones you would like to try!

1. Try a new activity

2. Try a new food

3. Ask friends or family silly questions

4. Look up new hobbies

5. Video chat with someone

6. Try playing your favorite game without any words

7. Play charades

8. Act out your favorite tv shows

9. Sing karaoke

10. Create something (wood, arts and crafts)

11. Call friends or family and ask them to tell you stories about their past

12. Create a new game or obstacle course in or outside your home

13. Video work out with friends

14. Build a tent or fort

15. Try learning to make a new recipe

16. Research an interest

17. Find a way to help someone you live with

18. Do a video scavenger with friends

19. Draw a comic strip or write a story

20. Make lists of top things that make you happy

21. Create a fun game to play indoors

22. Take a relaxing bath

23. Take time to reflect on your goals

24. Find things to organize or clean

25. List ways you have been successful

MOOD EVALUATION

This section is to work on responding to emotions. Our actions can affect our moods. Research supports that we cannot avoid our feelings (Hayes, Strosahl, Bunting, Twohig, & Wilson, 2005). If we do, it increases the duration and intensity of those emotions. Facing our emotions is critical to our future success.

Here is a list of ways you can face your emotions. Circle the ones you would be comfortable with. Keep in mind if you are not comfortable with any of the ideas on this list, it is important you come up with different healthy and effective ways to process your emotions.

- Talking to a friend about your emotions

- Journaling about your emotions

- Recording yourself talking about your emotions

- Singing about your emotions

- Playing a musical instrument

- Drawing

- Other _____

Here is a list of counterproductive ways to respond to emotions. Check the ones that you sometimes use. Recognizing unhealthy ways you deal with emotions can help you stop those habits and improve your relationships and life.

- Be grumpy to friends or family
- Eat or drink to feel better emotionally
- Watch movies or play video games to shut off your brain and avoid feelings
- Sleep instead of facing your emotions
- Shop to avoid your feelings
- Invest in unhealthy relationships
- Isolate to avoid uncomfortable feelings
- Other _____

APPRECIATING THE GOOD

Increasing our awareness of the good is so important to our mental health. Often we downplay the good things in life and focus on the bad. We often say negative things about ourselves and say there is very little positive. Every person has value. Every person has reasons why they can feel good about themselves and their life. Teaching ourselves to notice the good can help us feel better about life. This worksheet is intended to help you get in the practice of noticing the good.

	SOMETHING I DID I AM PROUD OF.	SOMETHING I APPRECIATE.	SOMETHING HARD I WORKED THROUGH.
Sunday			
Monday			
Tuesday			
Wednesday			
Thursday			
Friday			
Saturday			

Self-esteem is something many people struggle with and can make depression worse. It's important to build your self-esteem by completing small achievable goals and purposely putting yourself in situations where you can succeed. If you don't know what your strengths are, ask a trusted individual to help you discover them. It is also important to remember we all struggle with things and have a room to grow. Accepting that no one is perfect is an important part of building your self-esteem.

List three situations where it would be easy for you to succeed:

Example: When I work on computers, I feel confident and effective because I have success with diagnosing the problem and finding a solution.

1. _____

2. _____

3. _____

CONCLUSION

Work through this chapter and practice applying the healthy strategies! Ask yourself the following questions:

- Did I practice the strategies multiple times per week that were discussed in the chapter?

- Did I have support from others as I worked on self-reflection and accountability?

- Would I benefit from going through this book with a trained therapist?

- Would I benefit from talking to my doctor about my mental health?

We hope this chapter was an encouragement to you and led to you moving closer to your values and fighting depression. ■

KATHERINE SAINT, PHD, LPC, BCBA-D, has her doctorate in Behavior Analysis and is a Licensed Professional Counselor. She presents locally and internationally on topics related to autism, mental health, and behavior analysis. Katherine has a private practice focusing on mental health counseling and is the Director of Training at Fox Valley Autism Treatment Program in Appleton, WI. She has designed college courses as well as published serval books and articles related to mental health.

CARLOS TORRES, BS is a published author, coach, and program director of a young adult program that helps people with disabilities live independent meaningful lives. In his free time Carlos coaches Miracle League, a special needs baseball team. He also creates curriculum and designs social skills groups for an applied behavior analysis program. Carlos leads sports groups for children and adults with disabilities, which has grown to over 100 people attending each group. He has worked with people with mental and physical disabilities for nearly a decade and has worked with more than 400 people with an autism diagnosis. Carlos' passion to help people with disabilities continues to grow!

TOOLS FOR STRESS MANAGEMENT

Raun D. Melmed, MD, FAAP

Adapted from
Harriet's Monster Diary: Awfully Anxious (But I Squish It, Big Time)

Stress is probably the common mental health challenge experienced by children in the 21st century. Stress itself is not good or bad—it just describes the demands placed upon us to adapt to our world and to various situations. A common response to stress in both adults as well as children is fear. Fear is a warning signal. It is our "fight or flight" system which prepares our bodies for action. That can be extremely helpful but at other times the system can go into overdrive. There are numerous reasons for that happening including environmental factors as well as biological predispositions. Some are capable of coping with and responding to these situations. For others, more is needed. It is strongly recommended that you discuss this with your doctor.

Most have choices about how to respond to stress and deal with fears and that is what this book is about. Parenting a child who is susceptible to worries and anxieties is a challenge, there are ways a parent can help.

Let's talk about stress and fear with our children. We know that talking about feelings help. Reassurance goes a long way. It is one of the cornerstones for nurturing parenting. Let your children know that you will make the world a safe place for them, that you will always be there for them. Maybe you can give them their own mantras or brief prayers to recite when stressed or nervous. Its surprising how many adults continue to use the words they learned from their loving parents in early childhood.

Let them know that sometimes we feel bad, grumpy, tearful, or upset—and we don't always know why. This can happen when we must take tests, or speak in front of the class, or go to a new place and meet new people. We feel scared and worried, and sometimes get a butterfly feeling in our tummies, and our heart beats too fast.

Tell them those feelings are called "stress." Stress is something which happens when we feel pressured or must do something which is new or different. Let them know feeling stressed or nervous are normal feelings and they can always be comfortable in letting a parent know when they feel that way.

The good thing is that we can learn to recognize signals of stress, and after that we can learn to do something about them. We will need the right tools to tackle this stress problem. We can call it our Stress Management Toolbox.

Just letting your child know you understand them and teaching them about the stress process can be so helpful. Knowledge is a powerful coping tool.

Parents can teach the two basic steps to the stress management process— regardless of age or ability. The first step is to say, "I feel." That is when we describe how we feel. We say that out loud—or at least use our inside voices to say it. We can learn to say, "I feel ..." and then describe how we feel, like "I feel stressed" or "I feel worried." Sometimes just saying "I feel ..." is enough to solve problems or at least to minimize them.

The second step is to say how we can cope or what we can do. That's when we say, "I can." Here we learn about tools that many kids use to cope with stress and fears. The child or adult must be able to say, "I feel." and after that, "I can ..."

LET'S START WITH "I FEEL ..."

Everyone, children and adults, experiences stress differently. Help children identify the way they feel when they are stressed. Some kids make their muscles tight like a suit of armor (like what happens if someone is going to hit you in the stomach). Some breathe fast or hold their breath. Others get tummy aches or even vomit. If muscles are tight for a long time they start to hurt—like a headache. If we breathe fast for too long, we might get dizzy and feel ill. If our stomachs are upset, we can get a stomachache.

Describing how one feels is an excellent way of getting in touch with our emotional state. For many children, these feelings can be overwhelming and mystifying and can lead to a stressed state. Once children can label these symptoms they have a way of getting in touch with their feelings. It moves the process from their gut and into their heads. They now have a chance to be mindful. So, if a child feels afraid with a thumping heart and a tummy full of butterflies it doesn't mean that a disaster will happen or that the sky will fall in. It just means that they are stressed. Then they can say "I feel stressed!" That's the message.

Let your child circle the things they feel when stressed:

Do you ever have these body signs?

- ❑ Head full of aches
- ❑ Tummy full of butterflies
- ❑ Heart full of thumps
- ❑ Hands full of sweat
- ❑ Face full of red
- ❑ Muscles full of tightness
- ❑ Nights full of scares

Are you the kind of kid who has inside upsets like?

- ❑ Feeling afraid and worried
- ❑ Feeling sad and tearful
- ❑ Feeling mad and irritable
- ❑ Feeling shy

At school, do you?

- ❑ Get scared of talking in front of the class
- ❑ Forget things
- ❑ Feel picked on

❑ Take jokes too seriously

❑ Worry if people like you

If your child has some of these it may mean that they are stressed. Once again, let them say it say it "I am stressed."

"I CAN ..."

Good! Now that your child has learned about stress signals, the next step to learn is what to do about them. This is the second step to stress management. The "I can ..." step. This is where we figure out what the best stress management tools that will work for your child.

Teaching breath awareness, body awareness and mind awareness are three tools that help children manage stress. Here's how:

Breath awareness:

- Take a slow, deep breath.

- Breathe in all the way and then slowly breathe out.

- Feel your body relax.

- Count to 4 as you breathe in, then count to 4 as you breathe out.

- Do this 5 times. Even doing it one time helps your body relax.

Body awareness:

- Tighten the muscles in your face.

- Squeeze your eyes tight, bite your teeth tight. Hold this for 3 seconds.

- Relax those muscles and feel the difference in your face. Do this 3 times.

- Now tighten your fists, arms and stomach. Hold for 3 seconds and relax. Do this 3 times.

- Squeeze your legs together and point your toes. Hold for 3 seconds, and relax

- Repeat the exercise three times. *How does that feel?*

Mind awareness:

- After you control your breath and muscles, it is time to relax your mind.

- Think of a nice, calm place. Maybe a beach or a forest, or even your room!

- Imagine you are there now. Pretend what that place looks like. Try to hear what that place sounds like.

- Tell yourself "I can control my body and my mind. I can calm myself down when I get upset." Say this over and over to yourself.

Practice these skills:

- Practice them once a day. Bedtime works well.

- Practice them at school, on-line or in the car.

- These tools you will soon help you handle stressful times.

- Some tools might work better than others. Which do you like best?

ANOTHER TOOL FOR THE STRESS MANAGEMENT TOOLBOX— HARRIET'S STRESS "FUROMETER"

The Anxiety "Furometer" is used to combine the "I feel" and "I can" tools. It helps children grade or color code the level of their feelings and come up with coping tools they take from their Stress Management ToolBox to address each level.

- Draw a thermometer the shape of a test-tube with 4 sections.

- Let your child choose a color for the first section for when they are quite calm, e.g., green.

- Now chose the color they feel when they are beginning to get nervous— say yellow.

- The third section will be the color they feel when really stressed and the top level will be the color they feel when they are really losing it—say fire engine red!

- Label each section 1, 2, 3 and 4.

On the left side of the thermometer, label a column of feelings. These all start with "I feel". Write down the feelings or body signs your child has for each of the levels.

Remember, just identifying the level or color of the feelings might be enough of a coping tool to head off the most major of meltdowns.

On the right side of the Anxiety "Furometer" draw a column headed "I can." These will be the coping tools your child has learned. For each level, come up with coping skills appropriate to that level or color of stress. They could range from Breath Control for level 2 all the way to taking a shower for level 4!

This is not always easy, but the project does not have to be completed at one sitting!

Routine and rhythms are often lost at stressful times—even our bio-rhythms. As your child learns tools such breath body and mind awareness, make sure to provide routine, diet, and plenty of rest. Activities that enhance rhythmicity are very calming. Playing music, swinging, biking and our favorite rhythmical sport, swimming. Any sport is a great stress reliever!

ST⁴

Another tool that Harriet the Monster, uses to manage stress is the ST^4 process which was introduced by "Marvin the Monster" and "Timmy the Monster" in earlier books. ST^4 is designed to enhance mindfulness and self-awareness. It gives children a tool for changing a situation through being mindful, thereby allowing them to have more control over their bodies and minds. They are engaged in the treatment process as team members and assures them that adults are on their side and that we do understand the challenges they are having.

The ST^4 process works as follows:

- Let your children know that they can learn the power to control their bodies, their arms and legs and what comes out of their mouths. Even their thoughts! That is empowering!

- Explain what a "formula" means. Like water is H_2O or oxygen is O_2. Use those as examples but if that concept is abstract, just stick to the numbers and letters

- Tell your child how Harriet uses ST⁴. They can keep the formula secret if they want

- They can learn to slow down and STOP what they are doing—that's the S in Stop. One S

- Now they need to TAKE TIME TO THINK. Count the T's—that's four, right?

- One S and four T's—That's why we say ST⁴

- Draw that formula on stickers or badges with ST⁴ emblazoned on them

- Place the stickers on backpacks, on folders, on computer screens, school desks, on the bathroom mirror!

- It can be helpful to tell teachers about ST⁴ as they might use it in the classroom as well!

- The teacher simply points to the sticker on the child's desk as needed

- Keeping it secret allows the child to develop a positive rapport with the teacher while avoiding any unnecessary humiliation by being called out publicly.

HERE IS A LAST TOOL FOR YOUR CHILD'S STRESS MANAGEMENT TOOLBOX— A RELAXATION EXERCISE WHICH YOU CAN READ TO YOUR CHILD.

Let's spend a few minutes together, focusing on how you can relax your body and gain control over your thinking. This is a good to do when you start to feel tense or worried.

Get as comfortable as you can, good. Close your eyes and take some slow and deep breaths. Take a deep breath in, and then pretend to blow out a long string of bubbles into the air. Take another deep breath, and slowly blow out another string of bubbles. Pretend to see the bubbles float off into the air. See how shiny and colorful the bubbles look.

Slowly take another deep breath and slowly continue to blow out bubbles. Feel how your body feels nice and calm. Feel your body's muscles soften, and how you feel more and more comfortable. You are now relaxed.

Tell your child they can practice taking deep breaths and slowly breathe out bubbles at any time. That will help them with any worries or stress. You can solve your worries with the tools in your Stress Management Toolbox. You are in charge of your body and how you feel.

Hope everyone is calm and relaxed! ■

 **RAUN D. MELMED, MD, FAAP**, developmental and behavioral pediatrician, is director of the Melmed Center in Scottsdale, Arizona and co-founder and medical director of the Southwest Autism Research and Resource Center in Phoenix. He is Associate Professor of Pediatrics at the University of Arizona and on faculty at Arizona State University.

He is the author of *Autism: Early Intervention*; *Autism and the Extended Family*; and the ST⁴ Mindfulness Book for Kids series including *Marvin's Monster Diary: ADHD Attacks*, *Timmy's Monster Diary: Screen Time Attacks!*, *Harriet's Monster Diary: Awfully Anxious*, *Marvin's Monster Diary 2 (+ Lyssa): ADHD Emotion Explosion (But I Triumph, Big Time)*, and *Marvin's Monster Diary 3: Trouble with Friends (But I Get By, Big Time!)*.

PART 2

INSIGHTS FROM THE SPECTRUM

TEMPLE in LOCKDOWN

Temple Grandin, PhD

The world has changed so much and so suddenly. For the past few decades my life has consisted of constant travelling and speaking, along with lecturing at Colorado State University and helping my students. On March 12, 2020 I arrived home from a speaking engagement and that was my last trip. All trips and speaking engagements were cancelled for the foreseeable future. On March 13 we had a faculty meeting, and the faculty were told the university was shutting down. We had to get our classes online immediately.

Fortunately, I had a good computer tech person and my student Dennis Wilson taught me how to use the online platform. It has been harder on some of my graduate students. One student had her project cancelled. Fortunately, two other students had just completed projects. The bright side is that three of my students will have good papers ready to submit to scientific journals by the end of the semester. Writing is the one thing we can still do as easily as we did before.

At the time of writing this essay, it has been over a month since the stay at home order. Today I am participating in lots of online discussions and video conferencing. I wish to thank Cheryl Miller and Mark Deesing who have helped and supported me. Mark is my designer for my livestock consulting business, and we have lunch together every day. Creating a new routine was essential, and these lunches are now part of mine.

The best thing I did was to put myself on a new schedule and create a new routine. I get up and have breakfast, then I make sure that I am showered and dressed for work by 8 AM. Doing this routinely makes me feel much better. I am now spending several hours a day doing video conferences. Again, creating this daily schedule was essential.

Many families have asked me what to do with all the cooped-up kids after they have a routine set up. I tell them to go online to Google and type in "Life on the International Space Station." This is good for both perspective and for ideas of how people live for a long time in spaces even smaller than your home. You will find videos showing the cramped living quarters and a toilet they all must share. The astronauts have a schedule of scientific work, free time, station maintenance, and lots of exercise. Every day they have a group midday meal. Even in space, the schedule is what everything else is built around.

As for my emotional state—people ask me how I deal with the fear of getting COVID-19. At 72 years of age, I am definitely at risk. I have read many papers on ways to treat COVID-19 and I have figured some things out. Seeking knowledge on how to solve a problem reduces fear. People need to stop squabbling and find ways to successfully treat severe COVID-19 that do not cost a fortune. Fortunately, scientists around the world are cooperating. This is a time where having a logical brain and being autistic may be helpful.

Since I am in the at-risk group for COVID-19, I have spent hours reading scientific journal articles on repurposing existing generic medications to treat COVID-19. There are cheap generics that may help. As a highly logical person, I am horrified that progress on finding better treatment is hindered by fighting and politics. People spend too much time guarding their turf instead of solving things.

Lets get together and solve the problem. ∎

TEMPLE GRANDIN earned her PhD in animal science from the University of Illinois and is currently a Professor at Colorado State University. Dr. Grandin is one of the most respected individuals with autism in the world. She presents at conferences nationwide, helping thousands of parents and professionals understand how to help individuals with autism, Asperger's syndrome, and PDD. She is the author of *Emergence: Labeled Autistic, Thinking in Pictures, Animals in Translation* (which spent many weeks on *The New York Times* Best-Seller List), *The Autistic Brain*, and T*he Loving Push*, co-written with Debra Moore, PhD. One of the most celebrated—and effective—animal advocates on the planet, Dr. Grandin revolutionized animal movement systems and spearheaded reform of the quality of life for the world's agricultural animals.

HOW TO COPE DURING LOCKDOWN

Sean Barron

Early in this national and international pandemic, I found myself wondering how I would have dealt with such a major life disruption had it occurred 45 years ago when I was a teenager with autism. I recall how even the slightest change to my routines at home or in school often led to tremendous, out-of-proportion anger and anxiety. Family members appearing at the breakfast table in the wrong order in the morning was enough to tremendously sour my mood—with carryover that sometimes lasted the entire school day. If a milkshake cup wasn't filled to the top during a trip to the local ice cream shop, I would refuse to drink it. So how on Earth would an event powerful and far-reaching enough to shutter schools nationwide affect my already precarious sense of mental equilibrium? It's tough to imagine.

With that in mind, a few weeks ago I decided to use Facebook as a platform to network with parents, professionals and anyone else caring for someone on the autism spectrum, as well as those on it who might be experiencing difficulties related to the pandemic and subsequent stay-at-home and social distancing edicts. I prefaced the post by saying foremost that I wanted to create a safe, nonjudgmental environment for people to share their stories—positive or negative—about how they have adjusted to this unprecedented interruption to everyone's daily lives.

As I had expected, the results were a blend of both. Some parents said their children were doing fine, having made the adjustments and "toughing" it out. Others, however, were having a much harder time because their children were acting out more frequently and for longer durations; one or two had kids who were nonverbal and under high stress, so figuring out the best course of action to help them cope with something they could neither control nor prepare for was further complicated.

I made it a point to address to the best of my ability each respondent's concerns by first imaging myself in their households. I formed a mental picture of each person's demeanor and mood, then offered what I hoped were sound and practical suggestions, not advice, to help them better navigate through these trying circumstances. I suggested to a few mothers who are homeschooling their children some best-practice ideas such as tailoring their homes and using time increments to as closely as possible align with their children's school day and create some structure and predictability that seem so elusive these days on a wide scale. If the child has lunch from noon to 12:30, have it prepared at the house during that time; if language-arts class is in the afternoon, then teach that subject around the same time, I explained.

Another key suggestion I made was to break the isolation that many on the spectrum feel under normal circumstances, let alone during a major worldwide crisis in which we're unable to visit friends, family and loved ones. One way to do that is to reinforce the idea that we're all struggling together with this thing. That approach also can open the door to greater closeness by allowing parents to share specifically with their children how the pandemic is affecting them—to say, for example, that they too are frightened not only by what's going on now, but about the unknown. Removing the sense of isolation may not change the source of fear, but it can drive home the message to the child or adult on the spectrum that their feelings are perfectly normal and that everyone—autism or not—feels similarly.

Some other thoughts I have regarding this topic include assisting those who think more visually. This can be done by creating any number of time charts, picture representations and other visual aids to allow them to move more smoothly through the new transitions brought about by the crisis. Such a technique can also include feeling words like "scared," "angry," "happy" and so on, to give parents a better way to monitor their children's emotional states.

Major crises always grow scary tentacles and offshoots. In this case, we've seen more than our share of terrifying predictions and projections and, mixed in, conspiracy theories. So, for watching news accounts on the coronavirus, I think it's vital to walk that delicate tightrope between choosing to be ignorant about what's going on and "overdosing" on media reports. In other words, watch the news incrementally and explain to children on the spectrum what is factual and known, and do so straightforwardly. Spare them—and yourselves—frightening predictions that are just that. Expending emotional energy on all the ancillary, unproven claims will inevitably increase one's stress level exponentially, and doesn't this pandemic create enough anxiety as it is? As I have told several people over the past several weeks, anyone can make any prediction about the outcome of a football game, but if the contest is merely 5 minutes into the first quarter, it's impossible to know how the game will play out.

Finally, if you're a person of faith, as I am, there's nothing wrong with prayer and meditation. I've been doing a lot of both and feel a deeper connection with a higher power and loving force. For the last two Sundays, I've attended, for lack of a better description, parking lot church services in which the sermon is piped into congregants' vehicles via a low-power FM station.

I feel strongly that this crisis will soon be over and that a higher normalcy in which we treat one another better will emerge. The foremost question I have is how long will it last? ■

 **SEAN BARRON** co-wrote *There's a Boy in Here*, which describes his personal challenges with autism. He is now a journalist, lives independently, and has co-authored *Unwritten Rules of Social Relationships* with Dr. Temple Grandin. Sean is a graduate of Youngstown State University and writes for *The Youngstown Vindicator*.

STAYING SANE DURING THE COVID-19 LOCKDOWN

Anita Lesko

Wow. It's been an emotional rollercoaster since back in December. I can still recall seeing news stories of that Chinese doctor who was the whistleblower of the Coronavirus out of Wuhan, China. I kept saying to my husband, Abraham, that I didn't have a good feeling about the virus. Then came the first death outside of China in early February. Then on February 29th came the first death in the United States.

My anxiety level on a good day is moderate to high. With this event unfolding, my anxiety grew exponentially with each passing day. I just knew it would explode into a global pandemic. I was getting frustrated with the World Health Organization to finally announce it was a pandemic. I knew that the war against COVID-19 would ramp up once that announcement was declared.

Then the virus began spreading across the U.S. I was terrified. As a medical professional who deals with critically ill patients on a daily basis, fearing I'd become one of them wasn't a happy thought. Over and over, I'd be getting stories of doctors, nurses, respiratory therapists contracting COVID-19 from being on the front lines, taking care of those patients, and dying. It was literally a paralyzing anxiety.

Then I got the news that elective and non-essential surgery would be suspended nationwide for 60–90 days, possibly longer. So, there I was, after 32 years of getting up at 2:30 AM each weekday morning, suddenly unemployed.

Until whenever things get back to normal. I know this was done for several reasons. One to conserve vital supplies like masks, gowns, gloves and other necessary supplies for the COVID-19 patients and their medical staff. Second was to keep staff and beds available for the projected onslaught of critically ill COVID-19 patients. And also, to not bring patients having surgery into a facility where there's multiple COVID-19 patients and risk them getting infected. Each operating room has the anesthesia machines. We use them during each surgery to place patients on the ventilator. In case there really would be mass numbers of COVID-19 patients, those operating rooms would become ICU rooms and the anesthesia machines used as ventilators.

Not only was I scared of the virus, but now I was out of work. The first thing I did for myself was to start maintaining a new schedule. Although, I decided to forgo the 2:30 AM wake-up and move that to 4:00 AM because it's better for your circadian rhythm to not wake up before 4AM.

For nearly the past year I've been wishing I had the time to launch a new career. This is exactly what I'm doing now! I've wanted to learn so much new stuff and do a lot of writing. Suddenly here was the time to do it all.

As far as the lockdown, well neither Abraham nor I had to adjust to that! Aside from going to our jobs each day, we love being home! And now Abraham works from home doing his same job as before, only now from home. Except for going out for groceries once a week, we are totally at home. Our sanctuary.

I only have to go out for groceries and animal feed. I wear several masks and put on gloves prior to entering the store. I have my debit card already in my outer pocket in a plastic sandwich bag, so I don't have to touch my wallet with my contaminated gloves. I wear a hat, as the COVID-19 virus can survive on your hair, skin, and clothing.

Once home, all the packaged goods get sprayed with a Clorox-water solution and wiped down. All fruits and vegetables get thoroughly washed in sudsy water and rinsed, then patted dry. That all takes place out in the driveway under the trees. Then I head inside to shower and wash my hair, and all my clothes then gets laundered.

Each day around 11AM we go outside from a 45-minute walk. It's a great time to get our dose of Vitamin D naturally from the sun. Getting exercise each day is an excellent way to decrease anxiety and increase your endorphins.

We've also meditated each day for 20–30 minutes. That also helps get anxiety down.

I've been a news junkie my whole life. When the pandemic first started unfolding in the U.S., I'd be looking at the news multiple times throughout the day. What did that do? Each time I pulled up the news, the headlines were getting worse and worse. And so was my anxiety. It affected my sleep and daily life. I quickly realized that wasn't healthy or safe. I forced myself to limit the news to once a day, only for ten minutes. I also forced myself to simply focus on the day at hand, and what I needed to get done. Once I changed my ways, I started immediately feeling better.

Using this time for yet another good purpose, we started a big garden. We planned it all, then get the supplies to build raised beds to plant in and got it going. Normally there wouldn't be time to do all this, but it was something we talked about doing for years. This was the perfect opportunity to do something new. It's not only fun, but therapeutic.

Another enjoyable thing is cooking together. Now is a good time for families to make mealtime a together time. Get the kids involved (keeping them safe!) and everyone work together to prepare the food and get the meal ready. It's also a great time for parents to not allow cell phones, tablets, any mobile devices at the dinner table. Instead, share the food and conversation like the olden days before such devices became mainstream. It's a great way to connect with each other. If someone is alone, and they have a mobile device, think about using it to talk to a friend or family member.

I also emphasize to others who are protesting the stay-at-home orders, wearing masks, social distancing, that each of those measures are helping to save lives. I've seen many individuals with autism protesting about wearing masks stating its violating their disability rights. That makes my stomach in knots. For the past 32 years I've had to wear a mask each day, all day, in the operating room! Do I like it? Hardly. But it comes with the territory. Now, wearing a mask (or a scarf, or bandana) can not only save another person's life, but it might help save your own life. It's only necessary when you are out in public.

There comes a time in life, like now with a deadly pandemic, that one must go with the flow. There's no time now to focus on the autism thing. It's time to hunker down and do all that is necessary for you, your family, and others to be safer.

You can visit me at *www.yourwfpblife.com* to catch up on my new career! ■

HERE'S A FEW BLOGS TO READ!

https://www.yourwfpblife.com/blog/2020/03/29/start-your-journey-to-great-health-today-ywheh-2jswa-w26nh-z66kh-rftny-zdfzw-w56eg-fewf6-8ax7a-ad-kdg

https://www.yourwfpblife.com/blog/2020/03/29/start-your-journey-to-great-health-today-ywheh-2jswa-w26nh-z66kh-rftny-zdfzw-w56eg-fewf6

https://www.yourwfpblife.com/blog/2020/03/29/start-your-journey-to-great-health-today

https://www.yourwfpblife.com/blog/2020/03/29/start-your-journey-to-great-health-today-ywheh-2jswa-w26nh-z66kh-rftny-zdfzw-w56eg-fewf6-8ax7a

https://www.yourwfpblife.com/blog/2020/03/29/start-your-journey-to-great-health-today-ywheh-2jswa-w26nh-z66kh-rftny-zdfzw-w56eg-fewf6-8ax7a-ad-kdg-xfcdc

ANITA LESKO, author of *Temple Grandin: The Stories I Tell My Friends*, is an internationally recognized autism advocate and member of Autism Society of America's Panel of Autistic Advisors. She was diagnosed with Asperger's Syndrome at the age of fifty. A graduate of Columbia University, Anita was an honored speaker at the United Nations Headquarters for World Autism Awareness Day 2017. She is a contributing author for numerous publications including the Autism Asperger's Digest and The Mighty. She lives in Florida.

EVERYONE, GO TO YOUR ROOMS

Bella, Evelyn, and Bobbi Sheahan

Bobbi wrote, with Dr. Kathy DeOrnellas, What I Wish I'd Known About Raising a Child With Autism *(Future Horizons, 2011), in which she chronicled the first five years of her daughter Bella's life, including how the family learned of Bella's autism. The pseudonym "Grace" was used for Bella (now 16) and the pseudonym "Lucy" was used for Bella's sister Evelyn (now 17) in the book, but Bella and Evelyn have requested that their real names be used.*

BELLA: The lockdown hasn't felt like a trauma to me; it's more like my family is joining me in my world. That part of it has been nice. But I do like my alone time too.

BOBBI: Bella liked to be home a lot before the lockdown, and when our world hit "pause," suddenly all of us were right here with her.

BELLA: When will these people get out of my house? Why are you always here? The cat and I want to know. We NEED to know.

BOBBI: She's kidding. Sort of. Is she kidding? Well, there's two pieces here. Bella got a lot of togetherness thrown at her all at once, and also, she needs her routines. Right now, we are all at home with her ALL. THE. TIME. Needing a routine isn't the same thing as being able to create one on command, though.

BELLA: That's exactly right. Life has lost its structure, and structure can't just be remade the way that the rest of you think it can.

EVELYN: Before all this, whenever her routine was disrupted in a small way, such as me driving her someplace instead of our mom, she would be shaken for the rest of the day. While all of us have abruptly lost some things, like going to class every day and karate class in the evenings, she has abruptly lost the things that held life down for her like tent pegs.

BELLA: I want a routine, but not a made-up routine.

EVELYN: Additionally, this lockdown has meant that she's lost some of her coping mechanisms. There is a park near our house that has a swing set. For as long as I can remember, when she's stressed, she's gone to swing. We've had various swing sets built for her in our backyard, but since she is 16 now and hella tall, it's become near impossible to find any for her, so we've tried to help her find other coping mechanisms, which have been moderately successful.

BELLA: I think that the lockdown may have finally broken my attachment to the swings. I have replaced it with using the indoor exercise bike, doing more puzzles at home, and mostly walking Dobby, our dog.

BOBBI: Bella has been using the swings as a stress reliever since she could walk, and the swing at the park served the purpose, but it also led to some awkward interactions with curious strangers, and I considered it a safety issue. I could never convince Bella, but when it was announced that public parks were off limits, that safety rule triumphed over Bella's habit and she doesn't seem to miss it at all.

BELLA: When it comes to the park and the swings, it's been out of sight, out of mind, because a rule's a rule.

BOBBI: What do you think things will be like once all of this is over?

BELLA: I don't think I'll go back to the swings, and I don't really picture the future in a concrete way; that's not how my brain works. But I am worried that I won't get to go to my classes in person in the Fall, and I fear that classes will still need to be online in the Fall. If it's safe, and that's what we have to do, then that's what it will be. But I liked having a schedule and would rather go to classes in person. It's good to know yourself, and I know that I just don't do online classes. Honestly, the process of logging on just seems so needlessly complicated and full of anxiety.

BOBBI: I want to comment on the school and busy-ness piece. Our experience has taught us that online classes are a disaster for Bella, and it would not be loving for me to push her to tough it out and press through. We've crashed and burned with that under more normal circumstances, and we can't just demand such a high level of flexibility on short notice. OK, no notice. Her dislike of the online class format translates into anxiety and loathing for the logon process, and it's just not worth it to force her to go through it. We could drive ourselves up the wall wondering what aspect it is that makes it not worth it for her, but we just respect the fact that online classes are not her thing, and we will find another way. We have switched to totally homeschooling, with no online class-es, which presents its own set of challenges, but we're making it work. With no outside structure at all, we have had to create a schedule (which feels artificial) and use timers and incentives at home.

EVELYN: Something else that I think is noteworthy is the difference in the emotional impact that this is having on each of us. I love to be around people. Prior to this, Bella was working very hard to get out and connect with more people, not because she wanted to, but because my parents wanted her to have more social outlets.

BELLA: I didn't want to have much of a social life beforehand, so this is not too difficult. I know that my parents want me to socialize more, but that's not my priority, so it's nice to have a break from that. What I really want to do when the lockdown is over is to go to some of my favorite restaurants with my family. Evelyn wants to do more of the social, people-y things.

BOBBI: Life this way makes more sense to Bella. I think this lockdown has broken down the last of my efforts to "help" her to socialize when there isn't a reason or a task or a function that makes it worth it to her. Since all of her "social" life is at home for now, I actually see that she's found her voice a bit more; when the girls were small, we used to joke that Evelyn was Bella's spokesperson because Bella didn't talk very much. This lockdown has forced Bella to speak up more here at home and made it clear that each of us has our own distinct voice. I will be interested to see if that additional assertiveness and willingness to speak up will stick for Bella. I hope that it does. She likes people, but trying to understand social expectations and switch roles and rules in different situations with different people takes a lot out of her, and home is where she wants to recharge. And Bella is okay with being stuck at home since she intellectually understands the need for all of this.

EVELYN: Other than us being here with her all the time, this is her ideal living situation. For me, it's harder. I am a pragmatic person, but emotionally, I'm dying to get out of this and for things to go back to normal. Small irritations are exacerbated by the lockdown; for example, she typically speaks in a lot of quotes and pop culture references, and she gets frustrated (and so do we) when we don't understand what she's talking about.

BELLA: It's true. I have daydreams that I just completely immerse in. I don't want my family to interrupt me when I'm inside my head. And, as I have told my family many times before, the fiction I read is like a language to me and I enjoy repeating catchy things, which is also why I make pop culture references so often.

BOBBI: How do you think things will be different after the lockdown?

BELLA: I have no plans. I know that we will have to keep exercising a lot of precautions and social distancing for some time, so I am just going to go with it. That works for me anyway.

BOBBI: Bella needs structure to create structure, and what I mean is that there has to be a reason that makes sense to her. We did not understand how true this was until now.

BELLA: That is true. I do what makes sense to me. When my family wants me to create a routine, that seems pointless because I know that we have no place to go. I also don't feel the need to go to bed early, since we don't have anywhere to be in the morning. I do things according to the schedule or when I'm asked, but making the schedule is not something I do. I'd rather have a job with a clear schedule. And if what I'm doing is important, don't pull me off in the middle of a task to do something else either.

BOBBI: Not shifting tasks mid-stream is a biggie. Once you're focused on a task, I have to let you be, even if my hair is on fire.

BELLA: Well, yes.

EVELYN: When we were younger, I really didn't understand these differences. As her big sister, this used to make me angry because I felt as though my parents weren't pushing her enough. Bella does things that make sense to her, and some things are very difficult for her and she does them anyway because we ask her to. We see it as rigid thinking. She doesn't flex or read our faces to see that a situation has changed; we need to spell it out for her. She finds it nonsensical that anyone would ask her to make her own schedule when there's no place to go. There is no point in arguing about that. If she had somewhere to go, there would be a schedule.

BOBBI: Overall, Bella has taken the lockdown in stride, even more than the rest of us. At first, we thought it was just because she is happy doing less people-ing, but it's more than that. For Bella, the need for the lockdown makes sense to her, the rules are clear, and it helps us to cope. She doesn't worry about contracting COVID-19, focusing instead on precautionary measures, especially staying at home.

BELLA: The lockdown feels interesting to me, like the beginning of a zombie film, or pretty much anything that features an apocalypse. *Bird Box* feels especially similar, since even something as simple as a supply run at a grocery store can be perilous and requires us to wear masks. That's no problem because I understand what's expected of me. I'm not super-anxious about the virus because staying home can help lower our risk. I feel lucky that we need only stay home. It's not scary to me.

BOBBI: I have been somewhat surprised not to hear Bella express any anxiety about becoming ill, but she sees this in a very cut-and-dried way: we are doing what is within our control, full stop. To her, we are staying home and taking precautions, and we are not front-line essential workers, so that means we don't have to take risks, and thus we're not taking risks and thus it will all be ok. When I press her about the things that are not under our control, she doesn't really accept my premise. So that's it.

BELLA: We are doing what we can and being sensible, so we are safe.

BOBBI: Many of Bella's favorite experiences and things are here at home anyway, so she is experiencing it very differently. It helps that Bella enjoys our dog and our cat at least as much as she enjoys most people.

EVELYN: Yesterday, Dobby got grumpy with Bella and snapped at her. She didn't read his body language, and it hurt her feelings.

BELLA: I am just afraid that Dobby is starting to resent me a little for all the excessive walks. His little legs can only take so much.

BOBBI: It is interesting that you two even think about our 12-pound Chi-weenie's thought processes so differently. Bella's mind goes to the functional part: he's physically tired. Evelyn's mind goes to the interactive/communication parts: establishing respect and reading his signals. What are some other things we've learned about each other during this lockdown?

BELLA: We have always spent a lot of family time together, but during this lockdown I have explained several things about my routines and eating habits. For example, when I am made to eat foods I don't like, I chew on the left side of my mouth. If I like a food, I start on the right side of my mouth and I make sure that I have an even number of bites overall. Not stepping on cracks is standard (duh), but I like to step twice on each square of pavement. I like having an even number of steps, and an even number of letters in words. The fact that we have an odd number of steps in our house's staircase has always bothered me, but now you know this too. This revelation sparked a funny argument between me and Evelyn about whether or not the top landing qualifies as a step. Ever since I can remember, I have been developing a detailed system involving what letters I like and don't like and which letters I consider interchangeable and which ones I do not allow to end a sentence or story. When people are talking to me and they think I'm zoned out, it may actually be because they just said a word with a *c*, *g*, *b*, or *p*. I'd explain the significance of the differences between soft and hard *g*, but I don't think you could handle it and your brains might explode, and mine might as well, if I tried to fully explain.

BOBBI: It's fascinating to hear things like that, and it really does go both ways. This lockdown has helped me to see how some of our routines are just inexplicable and pointless to Bella. I also see how she works around our behavior to get her needs met. For example, when we are watching a movie that Bella doesn't want to watch, she will stay in the living room with us, but with headphones on and her back to the screen. She didn't do that before the lockdown. That's the amount of additional people-ing that she needs. Evelyn has persuaded Bella to play chess with her, and Bella jokingly says, "Is this a conspiracy to get me away from my brain and my screens?"

BELLA: My headphones and my alone time are important, but I see that I definitely need people. I don't need them in the same way that some other people do, and I don't need All the People at once. I like for my interactions with people to have a reason and I like to understand what's expected of me, and I don't enjoy being in large crowds of people, but I have thought about it a lot and I really like living with my family. I joke about my family being in my space, and I do need breaks from interaction with them, but I would not enjoy living alone through this lockdown. I do now know that I would not thrive living alone long term, and that has been a surprise to me. This quarantine has also helped me know more about what kind of job I want. Before the lockdown, I was ready to find my first job, but all of that is on hold. In the meantime, spending so much time indoors has led me to take a lot more walks, and I realize that I want to have a job that allows me to be outdoors at least part of the time. ∎

BOBBI SHEAHAN is a mom who teamed up with her child's psychologist to write her third book, *What I Wish I'd Known About Raising a Child with Autism: A Mom and a Psychologist Offer Heartfelt Advice for the First Five Years*. She wrote that book to spare other parents some of the pain, discouragement, and confusion that can accompany the early years of parenting a child who has or may have autism.

EVELYN SHEAHAN   ISABELLA SHEAHAN

PART 3

HOMESCHOOLING AND BEHAVIOR MANAGEMENT

HOMESCHOOLING YOUR STUDENT ON THE SPECTRUM:
START FROM YOUR HAMMOCK

Wendela Whitcomb Marsh, MA, BCBA, RSD

I f you're a parent of a school-aged child with ASD, you already know some-thing about homeschooling. You may have been homeschooling all along, or this may have come as a surprise when your child's school was closed due to COVID-19 health and safety concerns. Now that your family is sheltering at home, and you've learned to manage physical distancing, face masks, and frequent hand-washing, you realize that school may not open back up anytime soon, and you need to step up your parent-as-teacher game. Here are some tips to help you through.

First, go easy on yourself. Don't worry about your child falling behind ac-ademically. Everybody is facing the same situation, and no one should point a finger or blame parents if your child didn't do every worksheet recommended by your child's teacher. Your child's safety and happiness is your primary re-sponsibility and should be your focus right now. Love them unconditionally, hug them when they need a hug, and keep them happily occupied. Children learn all the time, not just when they're sitting at a desk with a book in front of them.

One thing children learn is when they're being lied to. It's not necessary to share every statistic that keeps you up at night, but don't say, "Everything's fine," when they can tell that you're worried. Knowing their grownups are wor-rying about something they won't talk about makes it seem like it must be too terrible for words. Their anxiety may spike as a result, and they may act out their confusion behaviorally. Some may start doing things you haven't seen in a long time, like bedwetting, babyish behavior, and two-year-old "tantrums" which are really autistic melt-downs. This is perfectly normal, and to be expected. Kids who don't have autism are doing some of these same things all around the world right now.

START

Your child's sense of security may be affected by a need for structure. This is something you can give them. You just need to START: Schedule Theme-based Activities at Regular Times. Why should you schedule activities at regular times rather than just letting your child do whatever they want whenever they want to? One reason is that a schedule is something your child is probably used to at school, and familiarity can be comforting. Another reason is that many children engage in fewer problem behaviors when they have a schedule to return to. Finally, a schedule is an anchor to keep them hooked into their day rather than floating aimlessly. If your child is perfectly happy to glide through their day with no set activities, if they create learning experiences for themselves, and if they don't have melt-downs that could be due to a lack of structure, then you may not need to schedule activities for them. However, many if not most children with ASD appreciate the comfort provided by knowing what they can expect throughout their day, and they do better when they have a schedule.

Why should your activities be theme-based? Themes help children cognitively link learning activities together. They often enjoy making connections and expanding their learning across subjects. Plus, it's fun to have special theme-based days to look forward to when you can't get out like you used to do. Maybe Pajama Day doesn't sound like much fun when they're home all day, but consider the following:

- Science Sunday (explore science through books or the internet)

- Museum Monday (find a virtual museum field trip online)

- Good Newsday Tuesday (read and report on, or write, only good news),

- Write your Friends-day Wednesday (keep in touch with classmates)

- Fursday or Purrsday Thursday, (pamper your pets or take a virtual trip to a zoo),

- Fan Fiction Friday (write a story about your favorite character from a book or TV show),

- Flatterday Saturday (flatter your family members, or flatten the curve by staying indoors,)

HAMMOCK

What kinds of theme-based activities should you plan? To ensure a range of types of experiences, plan activities around your HAMMOCK: Heart, Action, Mind, Music, Outdoors, Chores, and the Kitchen.

HEART

What do we mean by Heart activities? Think of activities that spark MATCHES: Mindfulness, Awe, Thankfulness, Charity, Helpfulness, Empathy, Spirituality.

A Heart activity that focuses on Mindfulness might be reading a book, such as Dr. Raun Melmed's *Monster Diary* series of Mindfulness Books for Kids, or *The Angry Octopus* by Lori Lite. Take a sightseeing trip around your block (practicing safety measures) to see how many animals you can see, or how many things in the sky, or how many things that are their favorite color, or that are smaller than their little fingernail. By focusing on specific things, your child (and you!) may increase your mindfulness of the world around you. Go on a Sense Walk, focusing on everything you can hear on one day, and on other days identifying things you see, or smell, or what you can touch on your walks. You can have Sense Walks around your own house as well as walking outside. Finally, practicing being still is a good mindfulness activity. If you have a snow globe (or can make one from a jar and glitter) have your child shake it up and then sit quietly watching the floating bits swirl and settle. If your child is too old for naps but needs some quiet time each day to keep from bouncing off the walls, Mindfulness activities may be just what they need.

Heart activities that inspire Awe are usually simple and free. Look up at the night sky and revel in the stars. Watch clouds moved by the wind, a spider spin a web, geese flying by, or ants on a parade. Virtual tours of planetariums or aquariums can be awe-inspiring.

Heart activities that promote Thankfulness might include writing or drawing thank-you notes to family members or community helpers, or making a "thank you" video to share. Make a "Compliment-Tree" out of a branch in a vase and make paper leaves. Family members can write complimentary messages for each other on the leaves and tape them to the tree.

Charity is a Heart activity that is perfectly suited to this time of sheltering at home. There are so many charities that feed the hungry, provide protection for doctors and nurses, and help the homeless. Your child may research what charity they would like to support and then brainstorm ways to support it. These may include starting or participating in a fundraiser, making face masks, sharing part of their allowance, raising awareness by creating a social media post about the charity, or even thanking a charitable organization or person for all the good work they're doing, expressing thankfulness and charity at the same time.

Helpfulness is a Heart activity that is similar to Charity, but closer to home. While charities help many people all over the world, being helpful is more of a family affair. Consider making a sticker chart, and every time someone notices another family member being helpful, they point it out, thank them, and put a sticker on the chart for that person. It's best not to label the stickers for any particular person which would promote competition and stress, but rather have a family goal to fill up your chart. The opportunity to put a sticker on the chart encourages children to keep their eyes open to notice when others are being helpful.

Empathy is another Heart trait. Activities that increase empathy include playing Someone Else's Shoes, where family members try on each other's shoes, and while wearing (or holding if they don't fit) that person's shoes, try to view the world through their eyes. Share what you think the other person might be feeling. Another Empathy activity is Freaky Friday, (based on the movie) where two people, usually a parent and a child, pretend to be each other all day.

Everyone calls them by the other's name, they wear articles of that person's clothing, and say and do the things they think the other person would say or do. Empathy can be the focus of reading a book or watching a TV show, by pausing to ask how they think a certain character is feeling, and why. If your child dislikes being interrupted, let them be the ones to choose when to pause the show or story and ask or answer the question about how the character feels.

Spirituality is an important Heart component. Whether or not your family has a particular faith, the pandemic is a time when you can focus on your personal beliefs and values. If you're used to worshiping in a church or temple, in addition to joining online services, let your child help plan a service at home. If you have moved and they miss their old church family, now you can join online worship services anywhere around the globe. If you don't ascribe to an organized religion, take time to evaluate what your family's spiritual priorities and values are. You don't have to be a member of any religion to grow spiritually in your own way. Sharing your personal spiritual path with your children helps them develop their own spirituality.

ACTION

Being physically active has been shown to be effective against anxiety and depression and to help sleep problems. When they aren't in school, your children don't have recess time or P.E. to go outside and get moving every day. However, you can schedule recess or P.E. at home, and provide a list of activities to choose from. These may include walking the dog, dancing, working out to a video, lifting weights or canned food, moving wet laundry to the dryer, riding a bike, creating an exercise video at home, or anything else they might come up with themselves to stay active. Consider downloading a free app of cheering sound effects to play when they complete an active task, so they can raise their fists, Rocky-style, and bask in the applause.

MIND

Your child's teacher has probably provided schoolwork to be done at home. Any school task works out your child's mind. If that math paper looks too overpowering, make a game of it. First trim it down to 6 or 12 problems, depending on how much you feel your child can tolerate. Remember that we are all under a lot of stress right now, whether it shows or not. For your child this may show up as being unable to complete a full page of math that they could do easily a few months ago. If you do 6 of the problems on the page, your child will have had a mathematical academic experience. Don't try to do 26 problems if your child becomes overwhelmed at the sight and either freezes or acts out in frustration. Better to have fun doing 6 problems. Here's how to play Random Roll:

1. Cut the math paper and put away the rest so your child only sees 6 (or 12) problems

2. Give your child a six-sided die (or two dice if you're doing 12 problems).

3. Have them roll the die/dice.

4. Whatever number they roll, they complete that problem.

5. Roll again and repeat until the paper is finished.

6. If they roll a repeat number, decide in advance what to do, which may include one or more of these ideas, or whatever your child thinks would be more fun:

   a. Check that problem using a calculator and correct it if needed.

   b. Raise their fists and chant, "I did it! I'm awesome!"

   c. Run a lap around the room while playing cheers on an applause app.

   d. All the above if they need longer breaks sprinkled randomly throughout.

MUSIC

Incorporating music through the day can relieve stress. Playing classical music in the background while working can be calming for many. Other kids will want to replay their favorite songs again and again and again. You can make a family event of a song by finding a "Sing Along" version you can play on your television or computer so everyone can see the words and join in. Consider declaring a Random Music Break, where you find objects in your house that can be used to make music or beat out a rhythm. Making up songs and dances is a great way to express feelings.

OUTDOORS

Just because you're sheltering at home doesn't mean you need to stay inside your home all the time. Follow the regulations in your area, but most communities allow walking around your neighborhood or visiting parks that remain open, as long as you practice safe physical distancing if you see other people, and wear your masks. If you have a yard, you have the perfect place to get some sunshine and fresh air. Ask your kids to make up their own versions of backyard scavenger hunts, relay races, hide-and-seek, and not-Easter not-egg hunts. Just because it's not Easter and you don't have any eggs to hide doesn't mean the kids can't have fun hiding and looking for other objects. Let them be creative, as long as they're enjoying some outdoor time.

CHORES

Nobody likes chores, but they must be done, so let's make them fun. Some families pay their children to take on extra chores. In addition to extra pocket money, your kids might take on chores to earn extra screen time, or the privilege of choosing what's for dinner tonight or what to watch on TV, or the chance to make a dessert for the family. Speaking of cooking...

KITCHEN

Kids in the kitchen are a recipe for fun as well as learning, as they read recipes and use math to measure ingredients. Making food is a life skill and working as a team cooking with other family members promotes social skills. Depending on their age and responsibility, you will need to be more or less involved, especially when using the stove or oven, but let your children take on as much of the cooking as they are able. They will have fun while they learn, and you all get to enjoy the fruits of their labors.

I know this is a lot to think about, but you don't have to do all of it, or any of it. If your kids are safe and happy, you're doing a terrific job! Worry less about academics and focus more on finding fun and making memories. You can do this. We can all do this together. ■

 **DR. WENDELA WHITCOMB MARSH, MA, BCBA, RSD**, author of *The ABCs of Autism in the Classroom: Setting the Stage for Success* and *Independent Living with Autism: Your Roadmap to Success*. She has been a special education teacher, school psychologist, autism specialist, speaker, writer, counselor, university instructor, and board-certified behavior analyst. She is the mother of two awesome individuals with autism, and was married for twenty-seven years to an amazing man with Asperger's syndrome. People on the spectrum, and the dedicated teachers who work with them, are among her favorite people in the world. Dr. Marsh lives in Salem, Oregon with her three children.

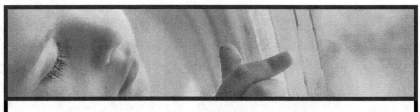

NOW YOU ARE
THE TEACHER...

Dr. Diana Friedlander

A few years ago, Dr. Burke and I co-authored a book for tweens, parents and teachers to help them better understand autism and how it relates to learning. One of our goals was to help kids become better self-advocates; to help them learn how to interact with their teachers and parents, to meet their unique learning needs. First, we taught them about what it means to have autism and how that could affect their learning. We then talked about the importance of awareness of their preferred learning style and, once gaining that awareness, how to apply it to their own learning through collaboration with their parents and teachers.

Times have changed, and the world has turned upside down. Teachers have had to develop new ways to teach their students, making use of every unique strategy they know and some they hadn't even dreamed of. Although parents are their children's first teachers, like never before, parents are being asked to engage with their children in this uncharted, potentially uncomfortable, distance learning. Parents have been catapulted into situations where they are forced to juggle many concurrent responsibilities. Many parents are teaching and working from home, all while trying to maintain a happy and healthy family living primarily within one seemingly ever shrinking space.

Helping your child to succeed at school is not a new concept for parents. What is new is that now you are the one overseeing that learning every day.

While reading these messages from our book will not make you an expert on preferred learning styles, you are already an expert at having a child with autism and you will be able to easily understand how learning choices affect your child. Often some simple changes in the way information is presented or received can deeply affect learning.

Your "preferred learning style" is a term which helps to describe the way in which a learner feels most comfortable taking in and digesting new and difficult information. Everyone has one, and generally we don't think about or label our preferred modality. However, for students who may already bring challenges such as lack of focus, poor executive functioning, rigidity, sensory intolerance, frustrations and the many, many learning issues we so often see in children with autism, it is essential to have a deeper understanding of just how information can be presented and received for maximum comfort and learning.

The term learning styles refers to the different ways we concentrate, process, internalize, and remember new and difficult information. When we use, rather than ignore, our natural learning styles, we learn more, more quickly, and with less frustration than when we try to use someone else's style.

For instance, one student might learn new information more easily while reading a complete book, while another student might prefer to hear their teacher talk about the new information before reading the book. Most people are familiar with the terms visual, auditory and kinesthetic learning. These are the basic modalities in which we present information. Teachers have become adept at constructing lessons which include many modalities, therefore more likely to reach more students. It is very important to understand that a student who perhaps learns best when manipulating numbers rather than writing them on a piece of paper or tablet will be more successful in their learning if they can access this accommodation. Lesson modifications need not be super involved, this student might benefit from numbers on post-it notes which can be easily relocated when working with a number line while working through a math problem.

Another example of preferred modalities might be listening to a recorded book rather than reading a paper or electronic copy. Teachers usually suggest students follow along to familiarize themselves with the text also, however, this activity can be very distracting to a student who learns primarily by listening. While special education teachers and classroom teachers are very adept at modifying their lessons to expand opportunities to access a student's preferred learning styles, school is now primarily a visual/auditory experience offered through the wonder of electronics and not all lessons are easily modified. However there are ways to ensure that the unique needs of your learner are being met.

Learning-style strengths are also affected by the learning environment. Each student may have a different preference for where it is easiest for them to learn without even knowing it. While concentrating, students react differently to the environment—sound versus silence; bright versus soft lighting; warm versus cool temperatures, and formal versus informal seating.

Students should ask adults to help them decide what learning space best complements their environmental learning-style preferences. For example, one might work best in a more formal space with desks, chairs, and tables. Other students may choose informal areas, such as couches, rugs, large exercise balls, soft chairs, etc.

Now you are understanding that everyone has strengths but that each person's strengths are different. Learning styles are based on reactions to many things in life, including feelings, routines, and events.

You and your student can best decide how to evaluate your work area so you will learn in a space that complements rather than tests their environmental learning-style preferences. By making simple changes in your workspace at home, you can create a space to work where they will feel most comfortable. Sometimes simple changes can make a huge difference. When the body feels comfortable and safe, the brain can concentrate on learning.

When you think about the learning environment, consider many things. One consideration is the level of sound in the room. Excessive or extraneous noise in the environment makes some people anxious and overwhelmed. Is your learner the type of person who prefers not to go to a movie theater because the sound is often turned up so high? This is a common thread among students who have autism. If so, you have probably figured out that streaming movies and watching them in a quiet, familiar space works much better, and everyone still gets to enjoy the movie.

Some people prefer to learn in an absolutely quiet environment. They feel that they lose concentration if there is any background noise in the room. If your learner is bothered by sound, perhaps he can wear noise-reducing earphones, change a seat to a quiet corner of the room, or use a cardboard study carrel (a good use for all those Amazon boxes) during tasks where he needs to concentrate closely. Other learners say background noise calms them and helps with focusing. In fact, experts have found that music can reduce stress and encourage creativity. Often people choose soothing classical music or even music with lyrics, however, that is an individual choice. A "white-noise" machine produces everyday environmental sounds like the sounds of a gentle breeze rustling the trees or ocean waves on the shore. Sometimes, such sounds can break up the quiet of a room and help learners to focus more on the task at hand.

Another environmental consideration is lighting. Bright overhead lights can feel harsh and over-stimulating to some, whereas a softer light may be too calming and cause a person to lose focus or even get sleepy.

Most school classrooms have overhead fluorescent light fixtures, but some schools offer alternative lighting. If your work room is brightly lit with harsh light, you might be able to make some simple changes. Sometimes a simple tool like a colored plastic overlay sheet placed on top of a page changes and softens the look of text enough to make it more pleasant to read. While they come in many colors, only trial and error will find the one that works best for your learner. When something is easier or more pleasant to read, the brain understands it better.

Sometimes sitting closer to a window, a natural light source, gives just the level needed. Others prefer a desk or table lamp which will create a softer and more gentle light.

Room temperature is another consideration. Everyone's body regulates its temperature differently. What seems cold to one person may be just right for another.

Clothing can also be an issue for some learners. If your child is one of those people, he probably feels more comfortable in looser clothing like sweatpants and loose tops. Even socks and snug shoes can be a distraction you can avoid with some careful thought. On the flip side, others might seek that nice secure "hug" that you can only get from Under Armour® or Spanx®. Some people say that feeling a slight weight or pressure to their clothing helps them to feel calm and collected. Often learners drape a neck support pillow around the shoulders or across the lap during work time to help them feel more grounded. These pillows are filled with sand, rice, or other weighty materials and can add that bit of pressure. Some are categorized as aromatherapy pillows because they are scented with lavender, vanilla, or other scents. The sense of smell is one of our most powerful senses. Different scents have a tendency to either calm or alert our bodies. This is a very individualized decision, so take note. When you are choosing a pillow, make sure that if it is scented, the scent is right for your learner or it can be more annoying than helpful. If you feel you need to heighten arousal, choose a scent that raises the level of alertness, if you feel your learner is too "pumped up" a calming scent may be in order. People with autism seem to be more sensitive than most people about what their bodies need to feel comfortable. Draw from your experience in addition to trying new things to help create a learning space where your student can do their best.

Learners can also be divided into two general categories, global or analytical. Knowing the difference will help you better understand how people learn.

Research shows that the analytic learner prefers to study alone for lengthy periods without interruption. They do not flit from one subject to another but are more comfortable seeing one task through to completion. They also focus on the parts which make up the big picture. For example, they might want to investigate specific job titles before understanding how the government works. These learners respond to a problem with logic first, instead of emotion. They solve problems systematically and logically, step by step.

A global learner might prefer to work on many tasks at the same time, moving between them. They can see the big picture or overall view and know where they are going. They are more likely to respond with emotion first. These are the students who can read that book from cover to cover without stopping to note or jot and then go back and make a complete outline! All this can happen while completing 4 math questions at the same time.

You and your child inevitably encounter pitfalls or challenges in your day-to-day lives because they have autism; however, with understanding comes power. You should now have a better understanding of those little quirky things that can lead to success or in a flash create complete shutdown.

You now know what autism might "look like" in the classroom and how it can impact learning. In addition, you have a better grasp on things you need to consider when helping your child navigate distance learning. You, better than anyone else, know what makes your learner successful and, conversely, what can ultimately lead to disaster. You have read about some practical suggestions and tools for changing learning patterns for manipulating the environment so your child will become a more comfortable and successful learner.

The old saying, "if you have met one person with autism, you have met one person with autism", cannot be more apparent in this context. When throwing preferred learning style into the mix, we create an even more unique profile. Students with autism can sometimes feel alienated and uncomfortable in their environment, both physically and emotionally.

A deeper understanding of how a student learns and basic, sometimes small, changes as to where and how he learns, may be the enabling factor leading to a successful lesson. ■

DIANA FRIEDLANDER, EdD, is the author of *Autism and You: Learning in Styles* and is an elementary special education teacher in Ridgefield, CT. She is also an adjunct professor at Western Connecticut State University (WCSU), Danbury, CT. Dr. Friedlander has taught students with autism for over 40 years in both private and public schools where she has been an advocate for the successful inclusion of students with special needs into the general education classroom. Her research investigated differences and similarities in learning styles of students with autism and their typical peers.

HOMESCHOOLING AND HOMEWORK:
HOW DO WE ACCOMPLISH IT WITHOUT BEHAVIORS?

Sheila Wagner, MEd

n all my years as an educator, I have always seen parents as a true collaborative member of a student's educational program. But now, with COVID-19 and schools closed, parents must assume the role not just as parent, but as teacher. These are two different roles and many parents struggle to get their child to see them in the light of a 'teacher' now. It is unfortunate that children across the nation are now at home during their normal school days because of COVID-19 and not at school. It is hoped that teachers are sending homework home for their children to do, and that they are using distance learning, computer generated lessons and zoom meetings to get lessons across and content learned. But many parents are still struggling with getting their child to sit down and do their work. It is a fact that many children with autism do not like to do 'homework', which unfortunately, is all the schooling they are getting at this time. They also can sometimes view the parent as only a 'parent', and not as a 'teacher' and resist their parent taking on this new role. During the quarantine, parents do not have the chance to send their child off to a school where trained teachers will receive them, daily schedules are predictable, and group actions can drive the work being done.

Teachers frequently see maladaptive behaviors from students with autism at school when it comes time to settle down and do the academic tasks. Now, parents are seeing this same thing at home. Students with autism frequently exhibit behaviors that baffle and frustrate our efforts to teach them. All too often, we (parents and teachers alike), try to control or eliminate inappropriate behavior without understanding its motivation. For the sake of this article, let us concentrate on the parents working with their child at home on their schoolwork.

Parents can get just as frustrated as teachers when behaviors do not shape quickly and should not feel bad about this. Parents may have great insight into their children, but do not have the objective viewpoint of the teacher. The teacher see this child in light of the other students in the classroom and have all the "tricks of the trade" learned from years of teaching. Parents can become so caught up in the cycle of trying to eliminate the interfering behavior that they can start eliminating work.

When this happens, the students can slip further behind in their studies. Too often the focus becomes stopping the behavior with the result that if the behavior does not stop the parents believe that they cannot teach their child. Reach out to their teacher to discuss the behaviors to see how they were handled at school. This may solve the problem entirely. If not, proceed with the steps below–you just may solve something that the teachers could not, or have not even seen before. If that is true, please share your results with the teachers when they are finally back in school.

Parents like teachers, need to understand that an interfering behavior is rarely exhibited "out of the blue". The function of the behavior is often apparent after analysis, and appropriate replacement behaviors can be found. I present the following steps as an aid to the parent when they face a difficult behavior that has not been eliminated by simple redirection techniques.

STEP 1: FIGURING OUT THE UNDERLYING CONDITIONS

If this behavior keeps coming back and cannot seem to be changed, then prior to tackling the behavior, the parent should not focus on the student, *but on him/ herself*. We already know that students with autism have severe impairment in social, language and behavior and we also know through research, that children with autism need a level of structure and predictability, concrete instructions and positive systems of shaping their behaviors. Can you judge if you are being consistent with your instruction of your child? Are you having your child do their homework at the same time each day? Do you have a schedule up on the wall that they can easily understand? Review all aspects of your instruction that is being given to your child to see if there are inconsistencies or areas that need change, prior to going on to the student's behavior. If an inappropriate behavior can change by making your instruction more efficient and easily understood by your child, the behavior may disappear, and you may not have to go further.

The next preliminary step is to consider *medical reasons for the behavior*. Remember, many parents tell professionals that their child rarely comes up to them and say "I just feel under the weather today," or "I really am sick to my stomach," or "My ear is stuffy and hurts." Behaviors often result because of medical reasons, especially those that come "out of the blue" or from nowhere. Take their temperature; feel their forehead; check to see if they have a runny nose or sore throat. Did they sleep and eat well last night? Make sure they have been given their medications that day (if they are on any). All of these conditions may cause inappropriate behaviors because children with autism use other means to communicate.

The final area for preliminary analysis is to *look at the environment*. Where do you have them doing their schoolwork? Is it in the same place every day? Is it at a table that must be cleared for meals three times a day? Is it near a window that can distract them? Is it near a hallway where other children can easily pass by them and maybe interrupt them? Are there overhead fans going that may blow papers or capture their obsessive interest? Look at all aspects of your house to find a quiet, non-distracting area that can be their "desk." Is a computer nearby for them to use, as well? In this time of isolation, you will want your child to continue to learn even if they can't do it in school so note any environmental conditions which may play a part in the inappropriate behavior.

After your preliminary analysis is completed and you discover that the inappropriate behavior is still there, begin a more in-depth look at these behaviors. After all, this child needs to learn, and behaviors should not be playing a part in their understanding of the content you are providing them.

STEP 2: IDENTIFYING THE BEHAVIOR

The second step is to define the behavior in objective terms. How would an *unfamiliar person* describe this behavior? How would your child's teacher describe it? How do others in the family describe it? Is it one particular behavior, or several all combined? What does it look like? Tear the behavior apart and look at the various components of it. A behavior component *must be seen to be described*!

STEP 3: PRELIMINARY DATA COLLECTION

The third step is to identify how often you are seeing this behavior happening. This will involve a bit of data collection. Teachers take data routinely on just about everything that happens in a school day, and most dislike it. But data taking does not have to be difficult; in fact, it can be easy. Grab a sheet of paper, draw some lines as shown below, and get ready to do just a little 'data collection'. You will be happy you did so as we go on.

Try to figure out a bit about this behavior. Does it only happen during schoolwork time? Is it happening at other times of the day? When? And how long does it go on? What activity are they doing when this happens? What do you think set this behavior off? By writing a description of the actual behavior and the consequence resulting from that behavior, you should start seeing some patterns. A sample form for this data collection can be as simple as the chart on the following page.

Start the data tracking as soon as you know that your efforts to eliminate the behavior by redirecting your child are not working. Take the data for as long as you can—maybe 2 to 3 weeks; even after you have figured out why your child is acting out. We should conduct data tracking over at least two weeks to gain a true insight. Less frequent behavior exhibition can be difficult to "catch," so longer data tracking periods may be necessary.

NAME: _____

BEHAVIOR BEING TRACKED: _____

TIME/DATE	PEOPLE AROUND HIM/HER	ACTIVITY BEING DONE	WHERE IN THE HOUSE DID IT HAPPEN?	WHAT SET THE BEHAVIOR OFF?	DESCRIBE THE BEHAVIOR	WHAT CONSEQUENCE DID YOU DELIVER?

STEP 4: ANALYSIS OF THE DATA

For teachers, it is helpful to have several other teachers look at the data to give some insight into what they have recorded. For parents, if possible, ask someone else to look at it and tell you what they think. Initially, this can be a spouse, husband, grandparent, older child, aunt/uncle, friend, or anyone that can help out. If you still have not gained any insight, then talk to their teacher, scan it and send it to them, take a picture with your cell phone and email it to them so they can help you figure it out. Often, a single viewpoint is not enough to find subtle patterns in behavior. Even teachers who are fully involved with the student sometimes do not identify functions of behaviors that an objective person might, so parents should not feel uncomfortable if they need help with this aspect.

Many times, you will immediately understand the motive or function of the behavior by looking at the data and changing the way you instruct them, the environment, their materials or other aspects of the schoolwork. But do not stop at this point. Now that you have the behavior figured out, you *MUST* go on to the next step!

STEP 5: "IF YOU DON'T LIKE THE BEHAVIOR..."

Your child is acting out for a reason. You have now figured out that reason. But if you dislike the behavior your child used to tell you what they wanted (whatever the function identified), **THEN WHAT DO YOU WANT THEM TO DO INSTEAD?** The behavior was exhibited for a *definite, legitimate* reason (for the child), so you *must* provide them with a different way to ask for that object (or activity, or whatever). If they had this new, more ideal behavior in their repertoire to get their wants and needs, they would have used it. Therefore, you must think of this as an area the student needs to be taught, "A Teachable Moment."

For example, if your child hits his brother or sister, or you, and the function was determined that your child felt you were too close to them all the time while they are working, then teach your student to tell his sibling or you to "please go away." This is the replacement behavior that is more acceptable and eliminates anyone else being hurt.

Many times, children with autism's behaviors are not necessarily negative in the broad sense, but just interferes with their work, such as leaving their seat and wandering around the room, reading books out loud, hoarding books, starting to undress in the hallway on the way to the bathroom, etc. These may not be "serious" behaviors, but they do not conform to what the rest of his class is doing (or may prove embarrassing) once he's back in school. Students with autism often just do not understand, or "pick up on" the more subtle cues that teachers or parents present and therefore "march to a different drum". Again, if you dislike the behavior the student is exhibiting, then what do you want them to do instead? (This is an ESPECIALLY important question which should be in the back of all parent's minds). Identify the opposite, replacement behavior that will need to be taught to the student.

For example, for the child that wanders away from his workspace at home, your replacement behavior is to stay in your seat for _____ minutes. Instead of reading books out loud, your targeted behavior becomes reading books silently. Instead of insisting on having 10 pencils on his desk, he may only have 3 at a time. Instead of beginning to undress on the way to the bathroom, teach your child that he will wait to get to the bathroom before unsnapping his pants.

"Targeted behaviors" take on a whole new meaning. You are no longer targeting the inappropriate behavior (though you will continue to track it with data collection). Instead, target the new, appropriate behaviors. The student's targeted behavior list should not include a list of his inappropriate behaviors, but should include the list of behaviors that are the *more appropriate* version. Handle the inappropriate behaviors when they come up, but target the appropriate behaviors for emphasis and instruction.

STEP 6: "OK, SO HOW, THEN, DO I GET MY CHILD TO DO THIS WONDERFUL, NEW BEHAVIOR?"

Now that you know what you want your child to do instead of acting out, now is the time to make sure that they will perform the better behavior that you have identified. How? By Demonstrating, Modeling, and especially, *Reinforcement*! Everyone changes their behavior when they need or want to. We know that children with autism often need to be taught specific replacement behaviors for their inappropriate ones. They truly may not understand *why* the new behavior should be exhibited instead of the old! After all, the acting out behavior was working pretty well for them. It got them out of tasks, and it got them tons of attention. Therefore, we must provide them with a motive for changing the behavior, whether or not they understand the reason, and we should definitely reinforce them for using the new behavior. If we do not reinforce the new behavior, why should they use it??

External motivators should be as close to the natural motivator and appropriate to the task as possible. However, sometimes that is not possible, and we end up looking for other motivators. In schools, we conduct motivational surveys which can provide a list of several preferred objects, activities, etc., that can encourage this new behavior. Parents can do the same. There are, essentially, 3 levels of reinforcers to choose from: a) *primary* (food, drink, warmth, comfort, etc.), b) *secondary* (checks, stickers, points, walks outside, etc.), and c) *intrinsic* (social attention, praise, pride in accomplishment, etc.). Many children with autism are unmotivated by the intrinsic level of reinforcers, and teachers (and parents) must look toward the secondary or primary levels to gain the child's understanding of why the new behavior is better than the old. Yes, some children with autism enjoy getting the praise from parents and have pride when they get a good grade. But if smiles, telling them they did a good job, hugs and kisses from mom and dad are not enough, then you will need to reach out to the secondary and intrinsic levels of reinforcers to pair with their replacement behaviors.

You also get your child to do "this wonderful new behavior" (instead of the behavior you objected to) by providing lots of opportunities to do so! They will not understand what you are teaching them or the reasons behind it if they only get the chance to do it once per day or week. If possible, set up as many opportunities to display this new behavior instead of the old as possible, so they may receive the reinforcer many times during the day. For example, Johnny gets Goldfish crackers when he stays in his designated desk after every 5 minutes. Another example is that Johnny gets a special sticker every time he completes one of the worksheets the teacher sent home. Only with repeated reinforcement of the new behaviors will your child begin to pair the two together (new behavior and the reinforcer). It will become more desirable for them to exhibit the more appropriate behavior than it was to exhibit the inappropriate behavior, and you now have behavior change! Keep up the good work!

SUMMARY

To summarize, the steps in changing your child's inappropriate behaviors at home include the following:

- Discuss behaviors with your child's teacher
- Preliminary Analysis
- Your own teaching instructions
- Consistency across all sessions
- Medical interventions/reasons
- Environmental conditions
- Identify the actual behavior
- Collect data
- Analyze the data
- Identify what you want the student to do instead
- Identify a motivator to encourage the replacement behavior
- Provide lots of opportunities to practice the new behaviors
- Problem Analysis

What if the behavior persists when you have completed all the steps above? It does not mean that it will be always be easy to affect the behavior change, even after completing everything above. So, what now? If this happens to you, ask yourself the questions listed below. Quite possibly, they will have the answer for you. Reach out to their teacher again and discuss all the steps you have gone through. Together, you just may be able to solve this situation.

1. If the behavior is resistant to all that you have tried, then look to the reinforcer. If the reinforcer chosen does not encourage the change in behavior, then by definition, *it is not a reinforcer.*

2. Is he/she getting enough practice? If your child never gets a chance to try the new behavior over and over again, then it will be exceedingly difficult to have them place this routine in their long-term memory banks. Reanalyze the opportunities and try again!

3. Are your expectations too high?

4. Are your expectations too low?

5. Are you using enough visuals to assist in the explanation of the plan?

6. Is the plan visually attractive (written for your *child*, not the *parent*)?

7. Are you analyzing the data frequently enough to give you results?

8. Am I targeting positive or negative behaviors?

9. Is your child actually being taught replacement skills? How and when? Can you use social stories (Carol Gray's work) to help explain it to them? (There is a lot of information on social stories on the Internet that is well worth looking up).

10. Is the plan too complicated? Maybe you are not implementing it the same way each time?

11. Am I tracking too many behaviors at once?

12. When was the last time s/he was reinforced by this plan (when was the goal reached)?

13. Are the reinforcers varied frequently?

14. Is everyone in the house consistent in conducting it?

15. Can your child look at it and intuitively know how they are doing during the day?

16. Does your child know what is being earned? How does he know? A picture?

17. Is the plan written in a parent-friendly, or student-friendly format?

18. What does the data show? Is anyone taking it?

19. Are you connecting with your child's teacher enough to discuss what is happening?

There may be many more questions to ask; puzzle it out with your child's teacher and keep trying. Learning the appropriate replacement behavior is ALWAYS worth it! ■

SHEILA WAGNER, MEd is a certified special educator who has been in the field of autism spectrum disorder (ASD) for over thirty-five years and retired from the positions of assistant director of the Emory Autism Center at Emory University and director of the Monarch School-Age Program. She is author of *Inclusive Programming for Elementary Students with Autism, Inclusive Programming for Middle School Students with Autism, Inclusive Programming for High School Students with Autism, Understanding Asperger's Syndrome-Fast Facts: A Guide for Teachers and Educators to Address the Needs of the Student*, and *Special People Special Ways*. Ms.Wagner has published widely in this field, including two books (for elementary and high school students with ASD), which both won the Autism Society of America's Outstanding Literary Work of the Year (2001 & 2010).

BUILD STRUCTURE FOR BETTER BEHAVIOR

Jim Ball, EdD, BCBA-D

F inding ourselves at home together with new rules, we sometimes find new inappropriate behaviors. When assessing reasons for inappropriate behavior, we need to make sure we have implemented strategies that build a structure for the person with autism. Ideally, we should build this structure before we implement a program.

People with autism like sameness. No surprises. The more we can let them know what will happen next, the better off we all are. The following are simple ways to structure the person with autism's life, while encouraging them to become more independent.

• SCHEDULES

Using a schedule is important. We all use schedules in our own lives and using one for the person with autism allows them to know what we expect of them, what they may earn for following the schedule and also helps them to predict the future.

We should make this schedule using pictures with words written under it, or just the written word alone (if the person can read). The person with autism should have some choice in what the schedule looks like. For example, if we know we have four programs we need to get done, we can put out the four programs and ask the person which one they want to do first, second, etc. This way they have some say in the order of the things they do. They often have such little choice in their lives; it is important that we allow them to assist with their schedule.

• WORK SPACES

Make sure that where ever you decide to work, you use the same place every time. This will help the person with autism know that when they are in this area, it is time for work. You do not want to do multiple things in this area, unless you have to. You want it to become the designated "work" area.

• MINIMAL DISTRACTIONS

You should have as little "stuff" in that area as possible. "Stuff" could be anything that will distract the person from completing their work. The more distractions are around, the harder it will be to keep the person's attention. You don't want to make it void of all things, but understand that the more that is around, the more things the person has to distract them.

• VISUAL CUES

All people with autism are visual learners. They watch how we do things and learn through repetition, doing things over and over again. Using visual cues helps them understand what it is we want them to do, as well as assist them in gaining independence. It is important they not have to rely on us all the time. If they know how to follow their schedule, all we may have to do is help set it up and they should be able to follow it, making them more independent.

• INDEPENDENT SCHEDULES

As discussed above, the use of visual schedules produces independence. This can be done quite easily; we only have to prompt correctly. For example, if the person with autism has three things to do, we can have pictures of the three things. Put these pictures in a photo album. When the person is ready, tell them to "go to work" and they go to their book, open it, look at the picture and complete the task. When they finish the first task, they turn the page and have a picture of the second task. They then begin to perform the second task. This will go on until they finish with all of their tasks.

• CONSISTENCY

The most important thing you need for good structure is consistency. You must remain consistent with your behavior if you expect the person with autism to be consistent with theirs. If the person does behavior *a*, always do behavior *b*. If the person does *c*, always do *d*. Once you have figured out what works, stick with it. If you react to behavior differently every time, the person with autism cannot figure you out. They will keep doing the behavior to see how you will react. So, once you have decided what you will do to deal with the behavior, remain consistent, and do the same thing every time. If you have designed the correct program, you will see the problem behavior begin to go away.

• PREDICTABILITY

Very similar to consistency, you must always be predictable for the individual with autism. If they know that you will do the same thing based on their behavior, they can predict what you will do. Their behaviors will begin to decrease based on them being able to predict how you will react.

• LANGUAGE USAGE

It is critical that when an individual with autism is out of control or displaying inappropriate behaviors at a high intensity level; we do not use much verbal language to calm them down. If anything, the more verbal language we use, the more we heighten their frustration or anxiety levels. We should use short language to get their attention and request they do something we already know they can do. For example, if they are out of control, we may just say, "Sit down" or "hand quiet" (if we know they already know these directives). Once they complete the first directive, we can reinforce that behavior and are more likely to get them back under control.

• ACTIVE TEACHING

Active teaching is nothing more than catching the person with autism when they are being good. Too many times when they are being good, we ignore them, not wanting to disrupt the good behavior. So what we should do is watch for those behaviors we want to see (i.e., listening, working nicely, following directions, etc.) When the person does the model behavior, we heavily reinforce this behavior, while trying to ignore or redirect the other behaviors we don't to see.

The keys to maintaining good behavior are all rooted in structure. Try implementing these structure rules and see how quickly behavior changes! ■

 **DR. JAMES BALL** is a Board-Certified Behavior Analyst and the President/Chief Executive Officer of JB Autism Consulting. He is also a member of the Interagency Autism Coordinating Committee as a public member. This committee, as outlined in the Autism Cares Act, makes recommendations to the Secretary on autism research gaps and submits to the Congress and the President an annual update on the summary of advances and to the strategic plan. He has been in the field of autism for over thirty years providing preschool, educational, residential, and employment services to children and adults affected by an autism spectrum disorder. He is author of Early Intervention and *Autism: Real-Life Questions, Real-Life Answers* and *You Can't Make Me! Pro-Active Strategies for Positive Behavior Change in Children.*

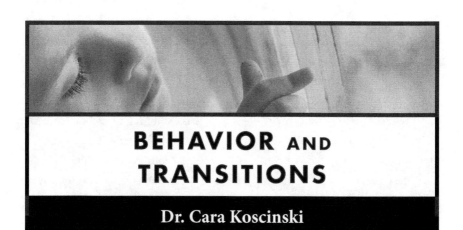

BEHAVIOR AND
TRANSITIONS

Dr. Cara Koscinski

My *Special Needs School Survival Guide* book offers help for families, new OTs, and teachers in the school setting. It's won a Family Choice Award and Academic's Choice Award due to the helpful information and use of non-technical jargon when explaining key concepts. The chapter discussing behavior and transitions includes information to help children deal with frustration and difficult emotions. Whether in school or at home, our children with autism require support and structure to avoid behavioral meltdowns. The changes brought about due to COVID-19 can be among the toughest for our children.

WHAT IS BEHAVIOR?

Often we think of behavior as a tantrum or action our child does to get attention. Behavior by definition in the *Merriam Webster Dictionary* is, "a: the manner of conducting oneself b: anything that an organism does involving action and response to stimulation c: the response." Children respond to their environment. From birth, we are bombarded with lights, sounds, textures, and touches. It is our response to these things (stimuli) that helps us to survive in the world. For instance, when a baby cries for his bottle, his caregiver feeds him. He learns that his actions have consequences and then either repeats them or tries something else. It is critical to remember that behavior is the student's way of communicating with you. (Koscinski, *The Pocket Occupational Therapist*, 2013)

When a student performs a "behavior," he is exhibiting a reaction to and an expression about something around him. It is important to note that society determines some unspoken rules as to what is acceptable and unacceptable behavior. The creation of rules is critical to helping our students know exactly what to expect in the setting. Classroom rules and expectations should be clearly posted in an area easily viewed by all students. As teachers, therapists, and caregivers, we have the responsibility to help our students to succeed in their environment. Oftentimes, frustration can lead to behavior issues. It is important to note that having any disability does not exclude a student from following the rules of the school and classroom. We cannot make exceptions for aggressive behavior. It's for this reason that we can implement a behavior plan in the student's IEP. However, when a student does not understand the rules, we have a responsibility to adapt the way we teach rules to that student. The adaptations will be discussed further in the chapter, but can often include auditory and visual cues.

DOES EVERY CHILD WITH SPECIAL NEEDS HAVE BEHAVIOR ISSUES?

You would be amazed at how often I receive this question. We all have behaviors! Some examples are scowling, laughing, stomping your feet in anger, crying, and yelling. As a parent of two children with autism spectrum disorders, I have the unique understanding of what is like to live and work professionally with children who have special needs. We have strict rules in our home and both of our sons are expected to obey them. Whether or not our children are verbal or non-verbal does not excuse them from following rules. Yes, it may be difficult to adhere to the social and unspoken rules, but the safety rules pertaining to the rights of the members of our home must be followed. The same is true in my clinics. Students are not permitted to hit, spit, or become aggressive toward our therapists. It is vastly different dealing with aggression from a 15-year-old than controlling a three-year-old with the same behavior. Many times, we suggest an aide or assistant who is uniquely trained in determining the specific student's signs of aggression and further how to keep the student and those around him safe. We have a safety plan in place with the numbers of those who are qualified to assist should the situation become dangerous. I recommend having a safety plan in writing and in place for all who work with students who exhibit aggression. The plan should be reviewed monthly and the team members should initial to confirm understanding.

Students with special needs and typical students sometimes cannot control behavior in the same way that you cannot control the knee-jerk reaction that happens during reflex testing. Some behavioral responses are simply reflexes. For example, when a person touches a hot stove, he reacts without thinking. Students with autism for example, may have difficulty communicating socially for wants, needs, and expressions of feelings and emotions. This may cause a decreased ability to communicate frustration and behaviors may result. If a child hears a fire alarm, he may go into a "flight or fight" response where he perceives the situation as dangerous. There are actually chemical reactions in the body, such as the release of the hormone adrenaline. As a result, he may flee the area looking for safety. He may also scream, push, or have an absolute melt-down. He simply cannot control this behavior as his basic instinct is for his own protection.

HOW DO I ANALYZE OR LOOK AT BEHAVIOR?

Children with special needs, those with sensory processing disorder, and typical children may exhibit behaviors that cannot be controlled. In fact, you probably have behaviors that result from frustrations in your daily life. What are some of them? Remember to consider your own responses to "difficult" situations or to things in your environment that cause you discomfort. Think about how you handle your responses. Some people chew gum or ice when they are frustrated, others yell or leave the scene to avoid the situation.

- Consider the following about your own behavior:

- How does my behavior serve me?

- Am I getting something out of it?

- Am I trying to escape something boring or difficult?

- Did my behavior get attention? Remember that sometimes negative behavior receives more attention than positive behavior does.

- Does it allow me to have some control over my life or surroundings?

- Am I in pain?

- What is good about my behavior?

- Am I trying to tell someone something (using words or not) with the behavior?

Students in the classroom may feel trapped as they simply do not know how or cannot express their frustrations. In order to assess a student's behavior, we need think further and spend some time being a behavior detective.

- Be objective.

- Consider the student's developmental level.

- Think about the student's environment.

- Could the student be sick? Remember the co-morbid conditions in Chapter 5?

- Is there an emotion that the student cannot verbalize, but is conveying through behavior?

- Are there speech and language or auditory processing delays?

- Is the activity when the behavior occurs a preferred or non- preferred task?

- What accommodations are in place to support the student's behavior?

WHAT IS A TRANSITION?

A transition is simply a change from one activity to another. A series of seamless transitions happens as you move throughout your daily routine, but you may feel disoriented on the first day of vacation or when in a new setting. Most of us can navigate the situation with some effort and transition smoothly.

Unfortunately, children with special needs may have great difficulty with transitions. For example, students with autism have difficulty with abstract concepts such as time. If a student doesn't fully understand the situation, he may have increased anxiety which may cause a negative behavior. The magnitude of the anxiety increases when a child cannot verbally express the fear of the unknown or about an upcoming activity.

Be sure to ease students into transitions by providing them with a warning. This could be a verbal or visual warning. Timers that "show" time with a reddened area are available and are wonderful tools for providing a visual cue of time elapsing. Sand timers are also good; however, finding one that's plastic is critical as my students have thrown their timers in anger. Holding up two fingers and verbalizing, "two minute warning" is helpful. Finally, providing partners for transitions works well for children who are social and are motivated by their peers.

WHAT IS AN ABC PLAN?

There are many students who have ABC plans in place in their IEPs. ABC is an acronym for Antecedent, Behavior, Consequence. The antecedent is the event that occurred prior to or just before the behavior. It can be how a task is presented, a transition, decreased attention from peers, a noise or unexpected touch while in line, a non-preferred task among many others. The behavior is the physical, emotional, or any noted change in the student such as a tantrum or full melt-down. C stands for consequence or what we do to deal with the behavior. Consequences may include: ignoring, punishment, removal from the situation, raising voice in disapproval.

It is extremely important when analyzing behavior to be objective and place your own opinions of the student aside. I am confident that there is always a reason why someone acts the way to do. It is our responsibility as caretakers, teachers, and therapists to determine the why.

Make a chart similar to the one on the following page.

DATE/TIME	ANTECEDENT	BEHAVIOR	CONSEQUENCE	WHY? (FUNCTION)

- Describe the target behavior.

- With whom does the target behavior occur?

- What internal/external events occur (antecedents) before the behavior?

- What consequences were given?

- What was the possible reason(s) or functions of the behavior?

It is important to consider what has and has not worked with the student in the past. This will require investigation by many team members, including previous teachers and caregivers. Working as a team will form outcomes by helping with consistency in implementing the plan. What are the parents doing at home to discipline the child? What are their rules and how well does the student follow rules at home? Analyzing the student's strengths and weakness can assist in planning. Finally, consider that children often seek negative attention. This happens when we pay attention to a bad behavior. For example, a student in an otherwise quiet classroom speaks out with rude comments and other students laugh at her. The teacher stops his lesson and asks her to quiet down. She is getting attention from both the students and the teacher by acting badly. We do not intend to reinforce negative behavior but by the sole act of paying attention to it (and to the student/child); we have done so. Ignoring the behavior is helpful, but not always possible. It is important to plan a non-verbal punishment, such as simply placing an X on a strike board or a cotton ball (or other quiet reminder) on the student's desk. Three strikes, and you've lost a privilege. (But please do not take away a student's recess; it may be the only time she has a chance to have a sensory break.)

WHAT ARE STRATEGIES WE CAN USE TO HELP WITH BEHAVIOR?

Knowing the specific learning styles of the students you are teaching is a first step toward working with their behavior. Providing the appropriate cues and instructions tailored to the student with special needs is the first critical intervention. For example, most children with autism spectrum disorders are visual learners. Verbally expressing the directions or rules will not suffice for these students. A visual cue will assist them in understanding exactly what is expected. There are many types of visual cues that can be created. Some teachers prefer to take actual pictures of the daily activities/items needed and then laminate them. The pictures can be placed in the order in which they will occur that day. As the student moves through the routine, he will either remove the picture or add a token to the schedule board next to the task he just completed. This idea can be adapted to each task. For example, if the task involves an experiment in science, the steps of the experiment can be shown visually either by written words or pictures. The schedule can be placed on the student's desk or used by the entire classroom to ensure the student is not easily identified.

When giving directions verbally it is critical to follow the following tips:

- Speak slowly.

- Give only one direction at a time.

- Make the direction short.

- Be specific.

- Tell what is expected, don't ask. "Begin writing" vs. "Are you ready to write?"

- Use a neutral tone.

- Exaggerate key words.

Most importantly, when the student does not follow a direction, ensure you follow through with the consequences that are predetermined. It is unreasonable to expect students to follow the rules if you have not been consistent in implementing the consequences. never try to teach a student during a crisis. Discuss the consequences ahead of time and review them often with students. Everyone throughout the student's day needs to be consistent in implementing the consequences and rules.

Token systems can be utilized to help reinforce behavior. A token system can be tailored to fit each student's specific needs. The student earns a token when he completes a task. There should be a goal to earn a predetermined amount of tokens to earn the reward. This is a great way to work on delayed gratification. We have adapted the token board for some students to rate their own performance on a scale. Red is not completed, yellow is incomplete, and green is completed. There are a pre-determined number of green boxes filled in at the end of the day to earn a reward. I have found that older students benefit from analyzing their own behavior and work. It helps them to become more responsible for their own behavior.

I also strongly recommend the "three strikes and you're out" rule. Make a board by laminating card stock or an index card. Place three Velcro tabs onto the board. Each time you give a warning, an x must be placed on the strike board. When three strikes are earned, the student has a specific consequence. It is critical that you review the consequence before the activity takes place so there's no debate if three strikes are given.

WHAT IS A PANIC RESPONSE, MELTDOWN, OR FIGHT-OR-FLIGHT REACTION?

There are many times when our students have an abnormal or panic response to something that is considered non-threatening to most. This may be a sign of SPD (Sensory Processing Disorder) in one or more areas. The body's amygdala is the center where we process emotions such as fear. Our amygdala can actually get larger when we have anxiety and more frequent worry, anxiety, or panic attacks. Since our students may have experienced frequent failed attempts at functional and school tasks, they may worry or feel insecure when attempting something new or at which they have previously failed. The fear of failure may actually evoke the amygdala's response and cause a feeling of panic.

The sound of a fire alarm is designed to jolt us into a "fight or flight" mode. This is our body's response to protect us from the harm of fire or smoke. However, when we have the "fight or flight" response to the unexpected bump of another student, sound of a fluorescent light, or when climbing onto the playground equipment, the student may be exhibiting an abnormal response. Again, it is our jobs to ensure that we are detectives and help to determine why a student is having a meltdown.

WHAT IS SELF-CONTROL?

The act of controlling your emotions and behaviors is self-control. There are many ways to help students develop this critical skill. It is important to remember not the chronological age of the student, but rather to consider the developmental age of the student. For example, if the student is 13 and in the eighth grade, but his emotional level is that of a 10-year-old, do not set your expectations for social skills to be that of his peers. Reading the IEP's evaluation report is critical to learning about the various tests that have been completed to determine chronological vs. developmental age.

OUT OF THE POCKET ACTIVITY

- Assign partners to solve problems together. Give a problem and let them figure out a solution. Learning from directly interacting with peers in a real-life setting is one of the best ways to teach skills.

- Provide timers to students that show how long

- an activity will take. Having the visual aid is a helpful way to show students something as abstract as time.

- Encourage students to wait for the attention of teachers and other adults. This can be extremely difficult for students with special needs. Develop a cue such as a flag the student can put up onto a Styrofoam block on his desk when he needs assistance. He must wait until you come to his desk and remove the flag. The physical placement of an item can give the feeling of control to the student.

- Work on an activity as a class, such as a puzzle. Complete a little each day for a designated time. When the time's up, the students must move on to something else.

- Allow older students to problem solve (with your help) while watching others. This could be done at recess while observing other students. Encourage students to observe others who are waiting for their turn or who are exhibiting self-control. When the student has mastered this skill, encourage her to try it out with her peers. Let her build confidence by actually trying the skill and do not intervene or take over. Afterwards, discuss the student's performance with her and make suggestions or offer ways to improve for the next time. Letting the student choose from different possible solutions is a great way to help build confidence.

HOW DO I CHANNEL ANGER APPROPRIATELY?

One of the first things we teach in our clinic and during consultations with teachers is to determine what anger looks like for the specific student. As I mentioned earlier hitting, spitting, aggression, or screaming at others are all unacceptable behaviors. When students are angry—especially those who have limited verbal skills—communication may become difficult and behavior is the way these students "speak" to us. Channeling this anger is the challenge.

- Begin by establishing what behaviors are appropriate. Make a list of the behaviors and work with the student to demonstrate acceptable behaviors.

- Create a story that details what anger is and encourage the student to tell you examples of situations in which he becomes angry. If he is not able to verbally tell you, make an observation chart for a month and note those situations in which he gets angry. Let him know what you've observed. In the story, place pictures and as many visual representations as you can. It is helpful to have the student make the actual faces of his feelings so you can show him exactly what he looks like. Review the story frequently (with emphasis on the acceptable behaviors) and hand the story to the student when he becomes angry.

- Create an "I'm MAD or ANGRY" cue or sign that the student can give when either non-verbal or when extremely frustrated.

- Create visual cues such as a laminated STOP sign, picture of the sensory or calm down area, or make a specific motion (or stop in sign language) with your hands.

- Provide a safe place for the student to go if his behavior becomes out of control or harmful. The location must be discussed with all team members prior to the event that caused the behavior and listed in the IEP. The student should know where to go and be familiar with the location. Make sure there are items there such as pillows, bean bags, calming lighting, or weighted blankets. Soft or relaxing music would be beneficial to assist the student in calming. Remember that no teaching should be done during a tantrum or melt-down.

HOW DO I MOTIVATE STUDENTS (ESPECIALLY OLDER STUDENTS) TO LEARN?

When children are entering school as kindergarteners, they may have an enthusiasm for learning that is exciting to teachers. As the years progress and the topics of study get more complicated and teachers expect more independence, the excitement of students may dwindle. As you may imagine, many students with special needs can become increasingly frustrated with school at this time. When my children were younger, I remember friends remarking, "Sure, it's easy when they're cute and little, but wait until they are bigger and things get difficult!" These comments resounded in my head as my children grew. There are many creative ways teachers and parents can motivate students throughout their educational journey.

It is our responsibility to provide praise and encouragement to our students. Every time they try a new skill, their success (combined with our response) can be critical for building confidence. We need to be good models of the behaviors we expect. When we are motivated to learn, it will be more exciting for our students. We should expect them to thrive and support them when they do not. Figuring out just how to do that is the trick.

- Encourage students to learn using a preferred topic. For example, it may be easier to work on a math word problem when we change the wording to a subject that is interesting to the child. Today, I adapted an algebra problem for my son (as I homeschooled him). Instead of using the reference to going to the dress store, as the original wording suggested, I substituted going to the football game. His interest peaked and he actually enjoyed finding the solution. In science, learning about density may be easier if we compare two train models or sports balls.

- Make your expectations clear and offer written or step by step objectives for the task. When the student knows exactly what's expected of her, the task seems less daunting.

- Ensure that each step has a clear starting and ending point.

- Assist your student in setting his own goals. Determine what motivates him to learn and what incentives he may need to achieve his goals. Self-monitoring is an important skill to learn early in life. Provide checklists as the assignment progresses.

- OTs have learned the unique skill of activity analysis. This simply means that we can break tasks down into specific steps and then adapt (make easier) the step in which the student is having difficulty. Activity analysis can be done when therapists and teachers investigate and determine at which point the student is not successful and begin one step earlier. Ensure success at that step and then move on to the next one. Provide praise and rewards as each step is accomplished.

- Take pictures of students as they are working in class on various subjects. Write an article for the school or community newspaper about the wonderful things your students are learning.

HOW DO I HELP OLDER STUDENTS LEARN WHAT MOTIVATES THEM?

When students have difficulty with verbal skills, they may have difficulty expressing their feelings and emotions on paper. I have found that offering a limited number of choices is beneficial as it alleviates confusion and frustration. Here's an example of a checklist I recommend:

STATEMENT	ALWAYS	SOMETIMES	NEVER
I enjoy school.			
I enjoy learning new things.			
I enjoy working hard when something is difficult.			
I wake up excited to go to school.			
I enjoy it when I do better than others in my class.			
I am happy when I'm learning a new skill.			
I think school is something that will help my future goals.			

As you may have noticed, the examples provided are for students who have an understanding of their emotions. The wording in the chart can be adapted to fit a particular student's needs. What is important is to determine if the student enjoys school at all and further identify what creative ideas can help the student increase his enjoyment of learning. ■

 **CARA KOSCINSKI, MOT, OTR/L**, is the author of *Sensorimotor Interventions: Using Movement to Improve Overall Body Function*; *The Parent's Guide to Occupational Therapy for Autism and Special Needs*; *The Special Needs SCHOOL Survival Guide*; and *The Weighted Blanket Guide: Everything You Need to Know About Weighted Blankets and Deep Pressure for Autism, Chronic Pain, and Other Conditions*. She founded two pediatric therapy clinics. As "The Pocket Occupational Therapist," Cara provides OT consultations, trainings, CEUs, and seminars on autism, behavior, sensory, and movement. Cara's own two children have autism and she has studied extensively in behavior, sensory processing, and movement integration training. Articles written by Cara have been featured in many publications including, *Parents Magazine, Autism Asperger's Digest*, and *Autism File*.

PART 4

ACTIVITIES AND OCCUPATIONAL THERAPY

IN-SYNC ACTIVITIES TO HELP KIDS COPE WITH BEING COOPED UP

Carol Stock Kranowitz, MA

Being cooped up to prevent the spread of COVID-19 is so, so hard, especially for kids with autism and their grown-ups. An antidote for cabin fever is sensory-motor fun. This means stimulating the senses to get kids touching and moving, seeing and hearing in engaging ways. Here are five "In-Sync" activities to help families incorporate sensory-motor experiences into their endless indoor days.

"RUBBER BAND HARP"

(from 101 Activities for Kids in Tight Spaces)

WHAT TO DO: Provide a cigar box (lid removed) and an assortment of rubber bands. The child can choose a few or a lot of rubber bands and stretch them over the box. Then, she can strum or pluck the harp to accompany her favorite songs.

Children with autism and SPD often have excellent—or even perfect—musical pitch, so "tuning" the harp may be fun to try. To make a plucked rubber band sound higher, pull it behind the box so it tightens in front. To make the band sound lower, pull it toward the front to loosen it. You can feel, hear and see how the bands behave differently, depending on how loose or tight they are.

This activity develops and enhances the tactile, visual and auditory senses.

"CRASH PAD"

(from *The Out-of-Sync Child Has Fun*)

To the overly energetic child who likes to jump and bump and crash, now is the time to say, "Sure!" After this activity, he will feel better and calmer. If, on the other hand, your child lacks energy, after you introduce this activity, soon the child will go for it eagerly. Almost everybody loves this.

WHAT TO DO: Together, gather pillows, couch cushions, sleeping bags and comforters, and pile them up in the center of a room. Move furniture away so there is a clear space all around the mound. The child then dives into the heap.

This activity provides deep pressure to muscles and joints, providing proprioceptive and tactile input. The vestibular system gets a workout, too, as the child runs and leaps through space.

"HUG ROLL"

(from *Growing an In-Sync Child*)

Rolling is an excellent way to get in touch with one's whole body. This activity is interactive, as it needs a second roller—that means you. It's an on-the-spot remedy for your child, whether she needs to rev up, stay tuned, or calm down.

WHAT TO DO: Lie on your back on the carpet, with plenty of space around you. Have your child lie on your tummy. Hug each other tightly. Slowly roll over and over in a log roll. Protect your child's head if necessary so she doesn't hyperextend her neck. Holding her tight, roll in the opposite direction. Roll over a couch cushion. Roll over a partially filled air mattress, for a funny, bumpy ride.

This activity develops and enhances vestibular processing, as well as proprioceptive and tactile input.

"LISTEN AND DRAW"

(from *The In-Sync Activity Card Book*)

Here's a way to get the kids up off the couch and standing tall. It's good for their posture and upper-body strength. It helps them learn to pay attention and respond appropriately to environmental sounds.

WHAT TO DO: Set up an easel, or tape paper to the wall. Provide crayons. (With a crayon, the child can decide whether to make a light or dark line depending on how much pressure he applies. A marker is easier to use but boring, because the color intensity is always the same.) Play music and ask your child to draw the way the music inspires him. Have him draw with the other hand or while standing on a sturdy box, or lying on his back with the crayon between his toes. If drawing is not his thing, maybe moving to music is, so put away the crayons and just dance!

This activity strengthens auditory discrimination as well as proprioceptive, visual and tactile processing.

"HAMMER AND NAILS"

(from *The Out-of-Sync Child Has Fun*)

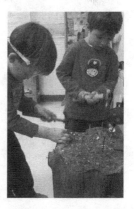

What better way to vent one's frustration from being stuck inside than by hitting nails? This activity lets children practice a valuable life skill in a safe environment.

WHAT TO DO: Get a tree stump, a can of penny nails, a real hammer (not a toy) and a protective face mask. Let the child hammer away.

If you think this activity is too challenging, your child can reap similar satisfaction and benefits by using a toy hammer to hit golf tees into a block of Styrofoam, an egg carton, or a pumpkin.

This activity improves visual skills (including binocularity, eye-hand co-ordination, depth perception and spatial awareness), as well as proprioceptive and tactile processing.

When the time comes that this novel coronavirus no longer rules our lives, children will still enjoy these sensory-motor experiences. Until then, stay safe, stay well, and have fun! ∎

Image credits:
Rubber Band Harp: C. Kranowitz
Crash Pad: T.J. Wylie, *The Out-of-Sync Child Has Fun*
Hug Roll: Durrell Godfrey, *Growing an In-Sync Child*
Listen and Draw: Durrell Godfrey, *The In-Sync Activity Card Book*
Hammer and Nails: St. Columba's Nursery School kids, permission granted

 **CAROL STOCK KRANOWITZ, MA**, is the author of *The Out-of-Sync Child*, *The Out-of-Sync Child Grows Up*, *The Out-of-Sync Child Has Fun*, and a children's book, *The Goodenoughs Get In Sync: 5 Family Members Overcome their Special Sensory Issues*. She was a preschool teacher for 25 years and helped to develop an innovative program to screen young children for Sensory Processing Disorder. She speaks regularly about the subject in the United States and abroad. In her books and presentations, she offers a fun and functional approach that integrates sensory-motor activities into everyday life at home and school. A graduate of Barnard College, she has an MA in Education and Human Development from The George Washington University.

KEEPING YOUR VISION in SYNC

Joye Newman, MA

O ne of the scariest things for me about this quarantine is the potential damage we are all doing to our visual systems by spending so much time inside, and so much time on our screens. We are limiting the ways we use our visual systems and ignoring the fact that our worlds extend past the distance from our eyes to our computers or iPads. It is especially detrimental to young children, whose visual systems are still developing. They are missing out on crucial opportunities for optimal vision development.

Vision plays a very significant role, often unrecognized, in becoming and being In Sync. Early visual skills emerge from strong tactile, vestibular, and proprioceptive sensory systems and continue to develop simultaneously with perceptual-motor skills—as long as we continue to move. Some essential visual processing skills are acuity, binocularity, and visual tracking.

The following is from my book, *Growing an In-Sync Child*, and may be helpful.

Acuity is the measurement of sight, most often represented by the ratio 20/20, which is considered perfect eyesight. A baby, however, comes into the world with a visual acuity of 20/200! This means he can see 10% as well as a person with perfect acuity. As he matures and begins to take an interest in objects at a closer range, his acuity should naturally stabilize at 20/20. Acuity is a measurement of sight only, and should not be confused with vision, which is the interpretation of what one sees. Some daily-life activities that require good acuity include:

- Recognizing letters and numbers

- Recognizing a friend's face

- Threading beads and lacing shoes

- Discriminating the corn in the succotash from the lima beans

- Sorting buttons

Binocularity is the ability to use both eyes together. This is crucial for depth perception. Any activity that encourages bilateral coordination also reinforces binocularity. You may see a child with poor binocularity lay his head on the desk or on his arm while reading or writing. When doing this, he is using only one eye to see. This habit should always be discouraged. Some daily-life skills that require efficient binocularity include:

- Playing hopscotch

- Judging distances

- Running accurately toward a target

- Holding one's head straight rather than tilting it to one side

- Stepping onto an escalator

Visual tracking is the ability to watch a moving target using only the eyes, with no head movement. Visual tracking develops as the infant begins to watch moving things such as a mobile or a parent. A child with poor visual tracking may frequently lose her place while reading, may reverse words, and may have mid-line crossing issues as the eyes fail to move smoothly from left to right (or right to left). Some daily-life skills that require efficient visual tracking include:

- Reading a sentence in a book

- Reading from the chalkboard

- Reading sheet music

- Playing ball sports

- Avoiding getting hit by a moving swing or car

(From Growing an In-Sync Child, *pp 17-20)*

Here are several activities that promote good vision development.

Look at My Hand

When handing something to your child, or when taking something from her, always be sure she LOOKS at your hand. Encouraging her to LOOK at what she is doing teaches her to use her eyes to direct her movements, while simultaneously improving her tracking skills. When you hand Sandra a toy, don't just put it in her hand. Rather, move the toy here and there a couple of times until she looks at what she is taking. When she gives you a toy, don't just take it from her; rather, move your hand here and there to make her LOOK at the toy's destination. Make it fun! "

How Many Steps?

This is a terrific exercise to do outside or even inside with a visual target such as a beanbag. Ask your child to look at an object like a tree or a parked car. Tell him that the game is to estimate (or "to guess") how many steps it will take for him to walk to the tree, making sure all his steps are the same size. After he gives an estimate, ask him to walk to the tree while counting his steps. You can change this around by asking him how many jumps ... hops ... tiptoe steps ...

I Spy

Play this game as often as possible, finding objects that are various distances from your child. Having him look farther away than the distance between his eyes and his screen is a great way to keep his visual system active.

Obstacle Courses

You don't need a long driveway in order to make an exciting obstacle course. It's possible to even create one inside. Follow these simple guidelines:

- Alternate over and under obstacles

- Think of prepositions: over, under, around, through, between, in, out

- Use various directions (walk backwards on this line, move sideways across this board)

- Use various forms of locomotion (jump, hop, slide, tiptoe)

Flashlights

Flashlights were invented for making children giggle. They are also highly effective for enhancing visual skills. Use them in any of these fun ways:

- Outdoors, once it's dark enough, shine a light quickly on an object. Hold it there for only a few seconds. Ask your child to identify the object you illuminated. Switch and let your child shine the light on something. The further away, the better for counteracting all that close visual screen work.

- Shine your light on a spot on the floor and ask your child to jump on it. Depending on your child's temperament, quickly move the light away (most children will giggle) or let your child rest there prior to your moving the light to a different spot.

- Give your child a second flashlight and ask her to shine her light on yours as your light makes a slow path along the ceiling or the wall.

During this time of quarantine, while we are all dependent on our screens, please encourage your children to move, look and see, so that when they can finally move through the world again freely, they will have In-Sync visual systems to help them navigate their way. ■

 **JOYE NEWMAN** was the founder and director of Kids Moving Company, which provides individual perceptual motor therapy to people ranging in age from 2 to 60 years. Currently, in addition to seeing private clients, she offers workshops to teachers and parents in perceptual motor development, creative movement, and reading readiness. Joye is a founding member of WISER, and served as the original Education Chair. Her other professional affiliations

include AAHPER, NAEYC and CEC. Joye co-authored the highly acclaimed book, *Growing an In-Sync Child: Simple, Fun Activities to Help Every Child Develop, Learn, and Grow*, and the *In Sync Activity Card Book* with her good friend, Carol Kranowitz.

THE 3 E's FOR **HOME** AND **SCHOOL: ENVIRONMENT, ENGAGEMENT,** AND **EDUCATION**

Beth Aune, OT/L

UNDERSTANDING AND CONNECTING WITH CHILDREN TO PROMOTE POSITIVE BEHAVIOR AND ACTIVE ENGAGEMENT

COVID-19 is changing how we live, work, attend school and communicate. Routines are disrupted. Home and school life are now commingled as parents have become educators as well as caregivers. Our children are confused and anxious and may exhibit an increase in challenging behaviors. Now, more than ever, caregivers, teachers and therapists face the daunting task of assisting our children to actively and willingly participate during their days. We can help by understanding what our children's behaviors are communicating to us, and to provide them with the supports they need, to promote positive behavior and active engagement.

First, what is "behavior"?

- A manner of behaving or acting
- Observable activity in a human or animal
- The responses to internal and external sensations and stimuli

When our children exhibit avoidance, distractibility, escape or refusal, we need to identify potential reasons, and make the necessary adaptations to assist them.

Some common reasons for avoidance, distractibility, escape or refusal are:

- Environment is not optimal
- Sensory challenges
- Decreased communication
- Shared engagement is not established
- Developmental readiness (cognitive, motor ability, language acquisition) is not established or clearly identified

General reminders and considerations:
Students with autism (and sometimes those without a defined diagnosis) exhibit:

- Increased distractibility and difficulty screening out extraneous stimuli
- Difficulty finding meaning in the environment and activities
- Communication delays or differences
- Poor organizational skills
- Decreased initiation and independence
- Short attention spans
- Processing deficits—visual, auditory, motor

It is necessary to create an environment conducive to promoting positive behavior:

1. Design an optimal sensory environment to provide a safe and calm space
2. Develop a predictable routine and schedule

3. Foster a positive and compassionate relationship with the child

Why is this important?

- Reduces challenging behaviors that impede interaction and learning:
    - Eloping and leaving teaching area
    - Inattentiveness and distractibility
    - Lack of awareness of routine and task demands
    - Sensory overload
- Promotes positive behaviors to stimulate engagement and learning:
    - Ability to follow a classroom routine
    - Increased attending to task
    - Increased active engagement
    - Achieving and maintaining a calm and alert arousal state
- A disorganized classroom or home space will:
    - Inhibit a child's ability to understand where he/she needs to be
    - Decrease a child's ability to attend to the tasks presented
    - Increase disruptive and maladaptive behaviors such as refusals, distracting peers, avoidance, and shut-down
    - Overwhelm a child's sensory systems, resulting in eloping, distress, aggression, shut-down (flight, fright, fight, freeze)

1. Creating an Optimal Sensory Environment

Our children often experience sensory overload, have difficulty organizing the sensory stimuli from the environment, and demonstrate challenges with modulating and discriminating sensation.

Visual Considerations

Our children may have difficulty organizing visual stimuli, may appear distracted and inattentive, or hyper-focus on visual details.

Visual Strategies

- Create clear physical boundaries to define centers and learning areas

- Work in a place that does not have visual distractions

- Reduce visual clutter—more is NOT better

- Put teaching materials within adult reach of each center for easy access and in closed bins or covered shelves

- Limit visual supports to those that are

  - Developmentally meaningful

  - Task and subject specific

Auditory Considerations

Adults need to consider students' language readiness and/or deficits and remember that communication challenges affect behavior. When we use too much language, talk too fast, don't allow time for processing, we can overload our children. They may appear to "not listen", and they may shut down (cover ears, eyes, look away). Our children may not understand our verbal directions, or they may misinterpret our communication. They may use their body to communicate, rather than their words.

Auditory Strategies

- Gain the child's attention before speaking

- Move closer before talking to him/her - try not to raise your voice across the room

- Keep language simple—do not over-talk

- Wait for a response—do not keep repeating the instruction

- Use visual supports to aid verbal processing (gesture, write on board, hold up a book)

- Have one adult give verbal instruction and a second adult model the desired response WITHOUT adding more language

- Use a modulated tone of voice—be aware of using a high pitch that is overstimulating

- The louder the child becomes, the quieter the adults must become

- Model and demonstrate. Children learn by watching and doing, not so much by listening

2. Develop a Predictable Routine and Schedule

This will assist to decrease anxiety and uncertainty. It will also promote independence and an ability for children to follow the routine without a need for excessive verbal or physical assistance.

Strategies

- Make a visual schedule tailored to your child's learning style. If your child cannot read, use objects or pictures

- Be as consistent as possible; have established times for getting dressed, having meals, school or therapy time, taking a bath or shower, and going to bed

- Begin by helping your child understand where they need to be, when they need to be there, and provide incentive to remain

- Do not begin with teaching new or "non-preferred" tasks—this will not stimulate your child to transition and/or remain in the teaching area

- Provide motivating and interesting tasks to promote active and willing engagement and participation

- Be patient and remember that your child requires much motivation, simplicity, repetition and positive reinforcement to learn a new routine

- Incorporate movement breaks throughout the day—be realistic about your child's ability to sit to attend

3. Fostering a Compassionate and Supportive Relationship

It takes time to develop trust and the sense of belonging. Children must first feel safe, understood, and cared about before following instruction and teaching can take place in an optimal manner. Observing and learning what motivates your children, what their strengths are, and what is uncomfortable or overstimulating for them is a pre-requisite for effective interaction and teaching. Learn about the way your children and students communicate, remembering that behavior is a communication—it is up to us as educators and parents to figure out what the student is telling us, and for us to make the necessary environmental, task, and instructional adaptations. Make learning fun to foster social interaction, to motivate increased joint attention, and to enjoy shared engagement.

Strategies

Reframing language we use to describe behavior can reframe our attitudes toward our children. Viewing behavior through a positive lens helps us to respond in a manner that better supports our children. For example,

Attention Seeking: Connection Seeking

- It is the basic human desire to connect with another human
- Think about the chronological and developmental age of our student
- Why is your child trying to gain your attention?
- What is the most likely way they will seek a connection?
- Provide positive attention by playing with or giving social praise

Ignoring the Behavior: Don't Be Reactive

- The danger of over-generalizing "ignore behavior" is that we inadvertently "ignore the child"
- We then turn our back and disconnect from the child

- We lose an opportunity to learn more about that child

- We lose an opportunity to teach a replacement skill

- That child lost an opportunity to be heard and respected

Say "No" to "No"

- Reflection: How many times in a day do you say, "No" or "Stop it" or "Don't" to your child?

- It is vital to pair a "no" with a "yes"

- Take time to demonstrate and practice the "right way" to behave (the "do over")

- Children can't just "figure it out" and change their behavior on their own

- Focus your attention on positive behavior

- Be specific with your expectation and be specific with your positive feedback

Push the "Pause" Button

- We do not always need to react or respond immediately

- Take time to watch and observe the child

- This allows us to use a "planned response" versus a "reactive response"

Be A Detective

- Go through a mental checklist:

  - Is the environment contributing to the behavior?

  - Is the child in a calm, alert, and attentive state?

  - Does the child understand the request?

  - Does the child have the skills to do what you are asking?

  - Is the student engaged and motivated?

Then, Modify Accordingly

- Make a change to the environment

- Provide needed sensory supports

- Gain the student's attention before directing or requesting

- Communicate in the most effective way according to that student's communication profile

- Simplify the task if needed

- Change the task or your approach to make it more interesting and motivating for the student

Encouraging and Helpful Reminders

It is much more beneficial to your children and students and less labor intensive for caregivers and educators to focus on promoting positive behaviors as compared to extinguishing negative patterns of behaviors.

Taking time and making the effort to establish an optimal physical and sensory environment, routine, and relationship conducive to learning will not only support your child's' progress; it will provide you, as parents and educators, with an encouraging sense of making a positive impact on your children's lives.

Children learn through play, and they are much more likely to exhibit sustained attention when tasks are presented in a playful and engaging manner. Play provides necessary sensory supports. We can incorporate academics into play; examples are sorting, categorizing, counting, labeling, sequencing, coloring, and writing. Hands-on and multi-sensory learning is often more motivating and engaging. Play fosters increased problem solving, creativity, and social engagement.

COVID-19 has been a challenging and disruptive influence in our lives and our children's lives. However, as parents, teachers, and therapists learn to adapt to this particular situation, we are also learning more about the children with whom we live and teach. We can embrace this challenge as an opportunity to more fully understand them, engage with them, and celebrate their unique gifts and talents. We can use this information to continue to help our children to feel safe, loved, understood, and honored. ■

REFERENCES

autismclassroomresources.com
educationviews.org
middletownautism.com
nspt4kids.com
simplypsychology.org
spectrumnews.org
special-learning.com
yourtherapysource.com

BETH AUNE is the owner-therapist of Desert Occupational Therapy for Kids, a pediatric outpatient clinic in Palm Desert, California. Beth and her team of dedicated and passionate professionals provide clinic and school-based assessment and intervention for at-risk children with a variety of diagnoses, including autism spectrum disorder, sensory processing disorder, emotional and behavioral regulation challenges, developmental delay, feeding dysfunction, Down syndrome, cerebral palsy, and others. Beth is a co-author of *Behavior Solutions for the Inclusive Classroom* (2010) and *Behavior Solutions in and Beyond the Inclusive Classroom* (2011) and sole author of *Behavior Solutions for the Home and the Community* (2013). She is a speaker throughout the nation on the topic of identifying and understanding children's problematic behaviors and sensory issues. Beth collaborates with educators to develop effective programs and provides ongoing supports and trainings to assist them to promote students' active engagement in the learning environment in self-contained special education classrooms, as well as inclusion in the general education setting. Her presentations, workshops, and books offer practical solutions and strategies for teachers and parents to implement in the school, home, and community settings. Beth and her team of occupational therapists are committed to help children achieve their highest potential in their daily function, with an emphasis on partnership with parents, caregivers, and teachers.

CREATING A SENSORY ENVIRONMENT

Nancy Kashman and Janet Mora

Adapted from *The Sensory Connection*

"The circumstances, objects, and conditions, by which one is surrounded, constitute the environment. The environment is any and all settings in which an individual finds himself."

With self-isolating, physically distancing, and people using a variety of masks and gloves, it's no wonder there is a need to look at current environments to assist individuals with sensory processing difficulties.

Safety of the environments being a top priority, properly safekeeping disinfectants and other sanitizing agents may be necessary in many households. Acclimating to the use of masks and gloves, by slowly introducing and getting used to the fit and feel could be another essential task.

Because we are facing a changed world, children who functioned fine previously, may now need extra support. Future environments, like schools, the cinema, possibly will also present new challenges.

Increasing understanding and awareness of the environment and making modifications may provide the individual with increased comfort, decreased anxiety, enhanced self-regulation, and facilitate learning.

Following is chapter six from our book, *The Sensory Connection: An OT SLP Approach*. It demonstrates more specifically the impact environments may have with our children and other individuals with sensory processing disorder and offers some guidance for addressing the difficulties.

Individuals with autism and other sensory integration disorders need strategies and tools that will enhance their ability to regulate their world and enable them to learn and participate in everyday life. Include functional and practical sensory strategies within the environment to ensure availability throughout the day.

The objective is to provide interventions that will facilitate coping strategies that decrease individuals' atypical sensitivities. The development and use of appropriate environmental strategies require adequate knowledge regarding the process of sensory integration by all interventionists.

ENVIRONMENTAL EFFECTS ON LEVEL OF AROUSAL

Dr. Temple Grandin describes some sensory input as painful and recommends that individuals with autism be protected from uncomfortable sensory input. If the environment is made as predictable and as comfortable as possible, the individual is better able to focus, learn, and interact. As the individual's skills and understanding improve, we hope that she can more readily deal with environmental stressors.

Be aware that people affect each other in the environment. How we move, how we speak, what we wear, and how we touch others impact everyone's level of arousal.

Triplets   *Jacob, Reanna, and Tyler are 5-year-old triplets. Although they were born at the same time, Tyler is not like his sister and brother. Tyler has autism and many sensory integration problems. Tyler's siblings do not understand what dysfunction in sensory integration is, but they live and experience Tyler's unusual behaviors on a daily basis. These behaviors can be funny, confusing, and sometimes scary.*

Tyler tends to put things in his mouth, so he is given special tubes to chew on at home. Jacob and Reanna never ask questions about the tubes, but they think it's fun to chew on Tyler's tube once in a while also. Sometimes, Tyler grabs one of his sibling's toys to chew on. This makes them angry. Jacob and Reanna are constantly reminded to put their little toys away.

Tyler has not learned how to talk yet, but he makes lots of noises. He sometimes sounds like a baby beginning to speak. He makes very loud noises that bother his brother and sister. The noise is most bothersome for them when in the car because it interferes with the music on the radio. Interestingly, noise bothers Tyler's ears, too. He walks around with his hands over his ears most of the time.

A note regarding Jacob, Reanna, and Tyler: The relationship among the triplets is ever-changing and developing. Tyler tends to wander, and Jacob has taken on the role of big brother. He is always ready to take Tyler's hand when he is walking away. Reanna currently appears to be less involved with Tyler, possibly due to his unpredictable behavior and his resistance to interactive play.

Tyler is fortunate to be growing up with siblings of the same age. He has constant models to learn from, and his siblings will be there for him when he's ready to interact. Jacob and Reanna will have a positive learning experience from growing up with a brother who has challenges. Even now, they are already showing signs of compassion and understanding of one another. At times, Jacob and Reanna see other children who may have something different about them, and they will ask questions about them. When they hear "just like Tyler," Jacob and Reanna understand and accept this. They are learning to not be afraid of people with differences.

When providing any new strategy, including environmental techniques, one should encourage, rather than force, an individual's participation. The individual often may require increasing exposure to the modification. Structure and predictability are critical; therefore, changes within a familiar environment should be gradual to allow the individual time to adjust.

The effects of the environment build. One may be able to tolerate some environmental stressors for short periods; however, as the frequency, intensity, or duration continues, the stress can cause a sharp increase in one's level of arousal. Fatigue or illness may also influence tolerance levels.

ENVIRONMENTAL STRATEGIES TO PREPARE
FOR LEARNING

Modifying the environment is one of the simplest and easiest tasks that professionals have found to be extremely effective in treatment. The table on the following page lists some of the more common arousing and calming environmental factors that can increase or decrease an individual's level of arousal.

In most instances, a calm environment facilitates attention and learning. Individuals in this environment are better able to tolerate the demands of learning and functioning.

Use caution in regard to interpreting an individual's level of arousal. An individual who appears hyperactive, or in her own world, may actually be in shutdown and not in need of any further stimulation. Shutdown occurs when the sensory information is so overwhelming that the individual basically tunes out any further input.

ENVIRONMENTAL EFFECTS ON LEVEL OF AROUSAL

OBSERVATION	AROUSING	CALMING
Auditory/Noise	Loud, sudden noises or voices, changes in volume	Soft voices, rhythmic music
Visual	Bright colors, excessive background stimuli	Muted colors, minimal background stimuli
Lighting	Bright or fluorescent lights	Soft, natural lighting
Room organization	Cluttered rooms	Orderly rooms with clearly defined pathways between furniture
Vestibular/Movement	Unpredictable, fast movements with sudden changes of position	Slow movements, rhythmic rocking
Tactile/Proprioception	Light touch, tickling, and unexpected touch	Pressure touch, hugging, moving against resistance
Temperature	Sudden temperature changes, temperature extremes	Neutral warmth
Odors	Strong or noxious odors (perfume, paint)	Soft odors (banana, vanilla) *all odors can sometimes be arousing

REDUCE SOUND DISTRACTIONS

Lower voices and decrease the rate of speech. Loud voices may get attention, but it is hard to "hang in there," especially when typical speech is perceived as shouting. This is an easy first step to calm an individual.

> *A parent told us, "Yesterday, after attending day one of your workshops, I tried lowering my voice when my daughter was having a meltdown. It worked!"*

Reduce sources of background noise—close doors when there is activity in the halls. Turn off noise-producing items, such as fans, electronic devices, televisions, and even air conditioning units (when possible). Decrease the volume on the cell or home phone.

> *At the age of ten, Pamela required a hearing screening for her school evaluation. Her appointment was on a teacher administration day to ensure a quiet environment. The audiologist's office was small and air-conditioned, with no windows. Pamela found it difficult to maintain her attention on the task. Her mother noticed that she would drift every two minutes, just when the air conditioner would click on. The audiologist moved Pamela to an empty classroom. Pamela was then able to complete the screening and passed with flying colors.*

- Use carpeting and ceiling tiles to reduce sound reverberation.

- Place tennis balls at the end of each leg to decrease the unexpected sound of a scraping chair.

- Secure foam with duct tape over the speaker to muffle the classroom bell or intercom.

- Provide an electronic device (MP3 player or cell phone) with earphones in noisy areas, such as a group home dining room, school cafeteria, or shopping mall.

- Large headphones provide proprioceptive input while tuning out external stimuli. If the individual is distracted by the music and resists earphones, explore using soft foam earplugs. Another option is "noise cancelling headphones," which actively reduce ambient noise.

- To decrease arousal, provide soft music at mealtimes to allow for a relaxing "dining" experience. Music that is 60 beats per minute, classical, rhythmical, or that incorporates environmental sounds is calming.

- To increase arousal for the individual who is lethargic or presents a decreased activity level, use fast music with an irregular beat.

Billy   *Billy, a youngster with a diagnosis of attention deficit disorder with hypoactivity, was unable to complete his meal within the allotted lunch period. Fast, rhythmic music increased his level of arousal and shortened the time needed for him to finish his lunch.*

Reduce Visual Distractions

- Cover bookshelves and toy shelves with curtains when the shelves are not in use.

- Place objects in opaque containers to decrease clutter while facilitating a need to communicate by asking for wanted items.

- Remove or turn over visuals when not in use to decrease visual clutter.

- Provide a study carrel or poster exhibit boards as screens on a student's desk.

- Avoid excessive wall decor and displays that hang from the ceiling and flutter. These are distracting and increase one's level of arousal. The same is true of the interventionists' clothing, jewelry, and hair. Bright or busy print clothing, hanging jewelry, and long hair can all be distractions.

  A parent told of her child's distraction with the university logo shirts her tutors wore. The parent provided long black shirts for the tutors, and this simple modification enabled the child to pay better attention.

- Display only what is immediately relevant to reduce visual clutter.

- Ease visual orientation by using contrasting colors, such as a dark mat on floors in front of a light-colored shower or commode. Contrasting colors during academics, such as placing a dark-colored paper under a worksheet, can improve the child's focus.

LIGHTING

Bright lighting and fluorescent bulbs often increase arousal level. The interventionist should be aware of her own position in relation to the outside light. Sun glare may cause difficulty for someone who is light sensitive, hindering her ability to maintain focus and attention. An individual who is light sensitive may benefit from sunglasses both indoors and out.

- Turn off unnecessary lighting.

- Use soft, natural sunlight and lamps with soft white bulbs.

- Cover fluorescent lights with swag sheeting.

Room Organization

- Keep rooms tidy and orderly

- Use dividers or painter's tape to define work or play areas; when possible, use an area for only one purpose.

- Arrange furniture with clear pathways. Poor sensory integration frequently affects motor planning, and this arrangement improves the ability to navigate by reducing visual demands.

Manage Vestibular Input and Movement

- Be aware of your movements and slow down—fast motion is stimulating to others.

- Speak to individuals at their eye level rather than having them look up or down. This facilitates communication because the individual can see the speaker's facial expressions and gestures.

- Consider limiting the need for individuals with vestibular issues to travel up and down stairs. When climbing stairs is unavoidable, travel when other environmental stressors are less.

- Secure any flowing curtains.

- Explore alternative seating (e.g., a rocking chair) to provide vestibular input.

Manage Tactile and Proprioceptive Input

- Avoid very light touch because it will increase arousal.

- Approach the individual from the front rather than from behind so that she can see the touch coming.

- Touch the individual firmly for brief periods of time. Never force touch.

- Be consistent with where the individual is touched; predictability may help tolerance.

- Provide space for the individual. The end of a line, eating at the end of a table, and "Kids Carry Me Floor Cushions" may all provide needed space.

- Make alternative seating available. This can provide calming proprioceptive pressure touch throughout the day. See alternative seating ideas under *Environmental Strategies*.

- Wash new clothing prior to the individual wearing it. The softer the clothes, the more comfortable they feel. Labels and seams may be irritating. Cut out labels and let individuals wear socks inside out when appropriate. When needed, utilize soft cloth masks. They can be washed and may be easier to tolerate.

Clothes   *Temple Grandin reports, "It took several days for me to stop feeling a new type of clothing on my body, whereas a typical person adapts to the change from pants to a dress in five minutes. New underwear causes great discomfort, and I have to wash it before I can wear it. Many people with autism prefer soft cotton against the skin. I also* *liked long pants, because I disliked the feeling of my legs touching each other."*

- Consider biker's shorts, tight sport shirts, or similar clothing to provide pressure touch to an individual who seeks this input.

- Install a hand-held showerhead at home to allow more control over the water.

Control Temperature and Odors

- Provide blankets for calming, neutral warmth.

- Provide neutral warmth in cooler climates by using flannel sheets.

- Be aware of environmental odors and the individual's reaction to them. Adverse odors may come from food, cleaning products, hand sanitizers, classroom supplies, or toiletries. Use unscented products.

- Do not wear perfumes or colognes.

Perfumes *A young woman with autism was in an elevator filled with people going to a television taping. It was obvious that everyone had primped for the possibility of being on TV—even for a moment. However, the scents were noxious to this young woman, and she loudly remarked to her mother, "It stinks in here!"*

ADDITIONAL ENVIRONMENTAL STRATEGIES

Provide a "Corner of the World"

Everyone needs an area to "get away from it all," particularly when wanting to relax from daily stress. This can be a special room in the house, a certain sofa, or a special chair. A "corner of the world," an area with minimal stimuli, provides a retreat for periodic breaks.

A quiet room, a classroom reading corner, a small tent, or a small child's swimming pool are a few examples. Incorporate various-sized pillows, beanbag chairs, gliders, or rocking chairs to provide calming proprioceptive and vestibular input. Eventually, the individuals may be better able to independently regulate their level of arousal by having an area to go to when needing to "chill out."

Alternative Seating

Various seating devices provide vestibular and proprioceptive input and, at times, boundaries.

- "Stuffed Pants"
- Beanbag chairs
- Soft, stuffed chairs
- Commercial air cushions
- Commercial "swim noodles" cut to provide boundaries on chair sides and fastened with heavy-duty tape
- T-stools formed from two pieces of wood fastened in the shape of the letter "T" to create a one-legged stool (requires balancing skills and increases vestibular input)
- Therapy ball or large beach ball (stabilized in a shallow cardboard box to prevent rolling)

Seating   *Learning can often be enhanced by utilizing alternative seating such as a therapy ball. An article by Shilling (2003) published in* The American Journal of Occupational Therapy *described a small study of 24 fourth grade students: 21 "typical" and three children with attention deficit hyperactivity disorder (ADHD). The children alternated sitting in regular chairs and on the therapy ball while participating in class work during language arts. Twenty-one of the 24 "typical" students and all of the students with ADHD stated that sitting on the therapy ball was more comfortable, improved their writing, and increased their ability to listen and complete their class work.*

- Rocking chair

- Hammock

- Glider

- Dycem® or nonskid material on a chair seat to provide additional proprioceptive feedback

- Thera-Band® tied between the bottoms of the front legs of a chair to provide additional proprioceptive input as a child moves her feet against the band

Kenny   *An OT and an SLP assessed four-year-old Kenny at home. His difficulties included a high level of arousal, frequent movement about the room, and a preoccupation with lining up objects rather than playing with and manipulating them. During the assessment, the therapists provided some quick environmental changes in an attempt to decrease Kenny's level of arousal and prepare him for task participation. This included lowering their voice volume, decreasing their speed of movement, and slowly swinging Kenny in a beach towel. A small booster chair provided boundaries.*

When Kenny was ready, the therapists gave him a motivating puzzle task. The therapists held the pieces for play in order to facilitate communication and engagement. Within a short time, Kenny signed the word "more," a task he had only infrequently performed.

The therapists provided the parents with a home program, which included environmental modifications and sensory-based tasks. One such activity included play with and exploration of sponge alphabet letters during bath time. This activity incorporated a highstress academic demand in a relaxing environment. Subsequently, the family reported that Kenny had lined up his alphabet sponges. He had lined them up in the correct order, had been able to identify each letter, and had even self-corrected errors. Previously, Kenny's cognition was considered questionable, at best.

Obviously, it may not always be possible to place a child in a tub to work, but modifying a child's environment and embedding sensory-based tasks that meet his needs throughout the day can better prepare the child for learning.

When prepared, relaxed, and attending, the child is able to access his knowledge and can show us his true capabilities.

Positioning, Positioning, Positioning

When looking at the environment, think about positioning of materials. Individuals with sensory integration dysfunction tend to have low muscle tone with poor trunk extension. Positioning of materials in a vertical plane or upright position can help in many ways.

For the speech therapist, placing materials in a vertical plane (rather than flat on a table) and encouraging pointing or reaching can facilitate extension of the trunk. With improved posture, speech therapy benefits include increased voice volume, and improved breath control, endurance, and stamina.

From the occupational therapy perspective, not only is the postural control important, it also facilitates the development of the shoulder, arm, hand, and wrist that is needed for fine motor skills. In this position (extension), the wrist is correctly aligned to develop stability, and it supports the appropriate thumb

Discourage "W" Sitting

position needed for developing dexterity. This in turn facilitates arching of the hand, which is needed for skillful manipulation of objects.

When working on the floor, encourage a variety of postures, including side sitting, prone on elbows, ring sitting, and side lying while propped on an elbow. Discourage "W" sitting.

Encourage working either in a sitting or standing position with arms and hands moving against gravity. Provide an easel, slant board, or book holder. Position materials to encourage slight reaching; this enhances the development of arm and shoulder muscles, trunk extension, and balance. Position objects on shelves, on the floor, or slightly out of reach.

Look at posture at desks and tables—elbows resting at about 90 degrees on the table, knees and hips at 90 degrees, and legs supported on the floor. When needed, phone books or stacked carpet squares can be used as foot supports.

Environmental Visual Supports

Many individuals with autism and sensory integration disorders are visual learners. Therefore, encourage the use of visual supports. Visual supports are concrete and static; they foster independence and responsibility, enhance self-esteem, and provide order, understanding, and organization to the individuals' often otherwise disorganized world.

Environmental visual supports include objects, pictures, symbols, and the written word. The selection of a visual support should be at the person's level of functioning and be as age-appropriate as possible. For example, a ten-year-old child functioning at a two-year-old level may do better when provided with a concrete object, such as a lunch box to indicate lunch, rather than a picture or the written word. However, be aware that when individuals are at an increased level of arousal, abilities frequently diminish and visual information may need to be at a lower developmental level.

When introducing a new visual tool, it may be necessary to demonstrate its use. This may initially increase the child's level of arousal. When the child is proficient, a visual organizer becomes a calming input in the environment.

Use visual supports across settings with all ages and developmental levels. Even though memory skills may appear excellent, stressors can tax functional memory, so cuing may be important. Effective visual supports decrease level of arousal, enhance ability to function, and minimize anxiety.

Supports   *At the age of ten, Pamela had to present a social studies project to her class. The presentation involved multiple tasks, which included public speaking and the use of props, both of which cause stress. Pamela successfully presented to her class by preparing a prerecorded speech. She was supported visually with a map that she pointed to as she played the tape.*

Well-positioned, clear visuals are essential. Avoid confusing and vague visual information. For example, visuals placed too high or out-of-range are difficult to use. Overly decorative lettering can distract from essential information.

The following are some of the visual supports that a person can successfully use in a variety of environments.

Personal Schedules/Calendars
Students should have daily, weekly, and monthly schedules. When appropriate, begin with simplified schedules and gradually increase complexity. Post the schedules on the wall, a desk, or have the students carry them.

Class and Home Schedules/Calendars
These give information about a day, week, month, or year. Be sure to sequence events within the calendar. Visually inform the students of changes in schedules

(e.g., posting the word "surprise" can replace previously determined events). Using a photo can prepare the students for a visitor or scheduled events.

Visual Routines

Visual routines explain the sequence of an activity or task (e.g., washing hands, brushing teeth, dressing). For example, photos of clothing or sequentially numbered baskets with items of clothing in each can facilitate dressing. Expand this idea and use it with classroom activities (e.g., an art project). These children often learn to read by sight; labeling can facilitate reading skills and increase vocabulary.

Labels/Signs

Strategically placed labels/signs on objects facilitate understanding and the expression of needs. At home, put the child's photo on the bedroom door to identify her room.

Lists

Lists can be as varied as a shopping list, a list of class materials needed for the day, or a list of family members' and classmates' phone numbers. For beginning readers and visual learners, add a photo of each person on the phone list. Use dry erase boards or paper to easily compile written lists. Encourage the child to use a list to retrieve needed materials, call friends, etc., to facilitate independence.

Sensory "Cheat Sheet"

A sensory "cheat sheet" is a visual list of activities, categorized according to the provided sensory input. Post it as a quick, effective reference for both the individual and caregiver. Activities should be specific to the individual and easily embedded within a daily schedule. There is an example of a sensory "cheat sheet" on the following page.

Bulletin Boards

Bulletin boards incorporate finished products of activities that a child is going to participate in during school. For the older student or adult, bulletin boards announce current or upcoming events, community activities, and daily menus.

Color Coding

The use of colors can clarify and organize one's environment. Supplies needed for a specific class may be easier to access when they are all coded with the same color. For example, all of the supplies needed for art class might be coded blue. A red stop sign on a doorway can often be enough of a visual prompt to stop a student who tends to wander. This, however, needs to be used in conjunction with a green "go" sign to indicate when the door should be opened to exit.

Joe   *Joe, a young man in his twenties, found it hard to verbally express his emotions. He devised a color-coded system to communicate to his mother how he was feeling. Joe wrote in red when angry, blue when sad, and yellow when happy. When his mother responded, she would use the same system.*

SENSORY "CHEAT SHEET"

TACTILE	PROPRIOCEPTIVE	VESTIBULAR
Dry beans, rice, or sand	Stomping or Marching	Sit in a rocking chair
Work with Play-Doh	Pull a heavy wagon	Run races around the room
Draw with shaving cream	Push chairs under table	Play parachute games
Massage with lotion	Help put away canned groceries	Jump on a trampoline or on the floor

Visual Rules

Visual rules assist the individual by allowing her to review rules of appropriate behavior as needed. Pictorial rules (e.g., "Quiet Voices, Quiet Feet, Quiet Hands") strategically placed around a classroom are an effective way to self-monitor one's behavior. Personal rules (e.g., lunchroom and playground behavior) can be easily seen when laminated onto index cards and secured by a ring or in photos taped to a desk.

Visual Markers

These markers provide information about one's own space, activity areas, and boundaries. For example, use masking tape on a large table or an easel to delineate individual space yet facilitate working alongside peers. Strategically place furniture around the room to create boundaries of activity areas, using gates as appropriate. ■

NANCY KASHMAN, LOTR graduated from the University of Wisconsin and has worked as a pediatric occupational therapist for over 25 years, in a variety of home and school settings. She emphasized sensory integration and neurodevelopmental treatment using a multi-sensory approach that is individualized to the needs of each child. Ms. Kashman also trained educators and therapists nationally in the use of sensory integration techniques to facilitate skill development. She is coauthor of *The Sensory Connection: An OT and SLP Team Approach—Sensory and Communication Strategies that WORK!*

JANET MORA, MA, CCC-SLP, is a graduate of Tulane University and is certified in speech language pathology, elementary education, learning disabilities, and school administration. She was the director of the innovative Chartwell Center in New Orleans and is an experienced speech therapist, classroom teacher, and student appraisal coordinator. She is coauthor of *The Sensory Connection: An OT and SLP Team Approach—Sensory and Communication Strategies that WORK!* and is also a nationally known speaker on using sensory integration techniques to facilitate communication skills for children and adults.

EXECUTIVE FUNCTION AND CHARACTER DEVELOPMENT IN LOCKDOWN: A SENSORY PERSPECTIVE

Paula Aquilla

I miss the beautiful smiling faces of your children in the clinic every day. I miss their happy voices bouncing off the walls when I am trying to concentrate, and I even miss them reaching over my laptop to erase the take home note I just finished!

I appreciate how hard you parents are all working, and I admire that you get up every morning and begin again—you are remarkable! All I can offer is my love and a few tips that I am using in my day to day life:

Grit: That "stick-to-it-ness" that enables us not to give up but to persevere on through these challenging times. Make a list every morning of three things you hope to accomplish and perhaps use a block schedule where you can organize your day. Different children can have a different colored block to organize. Stick to your list or schedule and you will have a feeling of accomplishment at the end of your day. Your grit and perseverance will pay off!

Hope: That this time of isolation will end, and we can return to our normal lives; better people because we have gone through this process. (Remember it takes tremendous pressure to change coal into a diamond!) Keeping a journal or a list of accomplishments and learning that each family member has gained each day can become a list of victories that can be reviewed each day or at the end of every week. This can build optimism and resilience in your children as they see that good things can come out of difficult times.

Innovation: Finding new ways to do things—new ways to connect and communicate with our loved ones, new ways to make meals out of whatever is in our fridge and cupboards, new ways to learn, new ways to plan our days—who knows? We may come up with better ways to do things that make our lives after this better. Keep what amazing things you have learned in your family journal so that you keep track of your accomplishments. Share what you have learned with others—you never know, it may just be what a person needs to hear!

Optimism: The positive way to view a situation; to look at things in a way that includes hope and the possibility of learning and positive change. Although it is important to acknowledge the negative as it it is a part of our reality, we have to balance it with optimism so that we can stay positive. What did you expect today? How did things turn out? Keep track of yours and your child's accomplishments. Build an optimism tree where each leaf has an accomplishment written on it. Fill that tree with leaves! Spring is here and buds are bursting from every branch—make it the same on your optimism tree.

Resilience: The ability to bounce back from hardship and disappointment and be stronger after the experience. This is certainly a time to bounce. If the day is overwhelming and you don't have an ounce of strength left—there will be a new day tomorrow; a fresh start, a chance to apply yesterday's learning to new challenges. Your children are watching you and learning from the wonderful example you are giving them. Getting up every morning, getting dressed and ready to greet the day. Pouring love into your meals and planning fun activities are acts of resilience. Demonstrating resilience is the best way for your children to learn this important skill.

Grace: Our children are watching us and learning from us. The position of grace is the position where we act in a way that respects and honors others. It is an easier place to be when we are calm and unstressed, and it takes more effort to maintain this place when we are stressed. We owe it to ourselves and our children to be the best we can be. Practicing self-compassion; showing ourselves understanding and patience enables us to be in a better position to show others compassion. Practicing self-care, getting your sleep, eating well, connecting with others, having fun, celebrating small victories, practicing gratitude give us the energy to be the best version of ourselves.

Patience: This time will end—it's just that no one seems to know when! We can't control the events around us, but we can exercise patience and focus on making our homelife as calm, fun and full of love as we can! Make your goals for the day and plan using your block schedule—this is an act of optimism and hope. Some days you will accomplish everything and some days, you won't. Be patient, there will be good and there will be trying days. Keep your chin up and take time at the end of each day to review the good points of everyone's day.

Gratitude: Our brain is an electrical and chemical organ. The chemicals, called neurotransmitters, change in response to our emotion, the sensory experience we are having or the demand we feel to do a task. Our thoughts can influence our neurotransmitters. Positive thoughts can release the neurotransmitters that help us feel good, enable us to think clearly and make good decisions, Thoughts filled with gratitude can influence our neurotransmitters and bias us toward feeling good. This weekend, make a gratitude chain with your family. Everyone has a strip of paper where they write what they are grateful for. Make each strip into a circle, creating a chain. You can hang your chain over your dinner table and "set the mood" for your meal.

Keep your journal of accomplishments and learning to review each day and end each day on a high note.

Please enjoy this adaptation of Chapter 7 of my book, *The Sensory Detective Curriculum*, to help you on your current journey.

Best wishes, thinking of you,
Paula Aquilla

When you drive past any school in Toronto, you will often see a character of the month on the sign in front of the school. The characters are:

- Respect
- Empathy
- Responsibility
- Cooperation
- Kindness

- Perseverance
- Fairness
- Teamwork
- Integrity
- Honesty

What a wonderful goal! Enabling students to develop these character traits sounds like a wonderful idea, but how do we do that? How do we develop character?

Character takes many years to develop. Research supports that self-regulation skills and emotional regulation skills, necessary for the development of character, continue to develop well into our early twenties. (Shankar Pg 33; ACT for Youth, 2002). Our character continues to develop throughout our life. Our successes and failures in meeting the demands of our environment help to make up our character. Our parents, family members, and teachers educate us on how to conduct ourselves. They provide the feedback we need, whether positive or negative, to help shape our character. There are no shortcuts to character development. It takes work, time, experience, honest feedback, and opportunities to try again.

The starting point in developing character is self-knowledge. Who is the person we would be proud to be? Who do we look up to? How do we want to interact with others? We have to know ourselves first. How do we work? What do we like/dislike? What environments do we succeed in? Which approaches work best in interacting with others? What activities are we best at?

The previous chapters of this book provided many opportunities to investigate and learn the answers to these questions. This learning is vital to children in discovering who they are, how they work, and what they like. Armed with this knowledge, children can set goals for themselves and make a plan to achieve them. How do you plan your life when you don't know where you're going? How do you know where you're going if you don't know yourself?

Character traits enable us to be aware of others in our group and to watch out for them. Our brains are wired to be social and character enables the maintenance of these social bonds. We understand that we are part of a larger group and when one of us is successful, all of us are successful. Character enables us to invest in each other; to take the time to understand another's perspective, to assume responsibility for our actions, and demonstrate respect and kindness for others. Character enables us to stick with a difficult task until it's complete—even if it's difficult. Character helps us to work on teams and be responsible to our fellow teammates. It supports honesty and integrity so that people in our groups can depend on us to do the things we say we will do. When we develop character, we develop a sense of who we are. We can predict how we will act in different situations, and develop a confidence in ourselves and an identity. These skills definitely prepare children for life in a society and help build strong citizens that can keep our society strong and unified. Character development is an excellent investment!

REVIEW OF SENSORY PROCESSING

In the Sensory Detective Curriculum, we learn that our sensory systems give us information about ourselves, and our environments. Sensory processing is working from the very beginning, feeding our nervous systems with information, even before we are born! With repeated exposure to sensation, the connections between the neurons become insulated and we become more efficient at processing sensations and executing responses. We learn about what sensations we enjoy. We also learn that some sensations can be difficult for us to process, so we can avoid those sensations. As we grow, we learn about our body and our environment and the world becomes a more predictable place. Efficient sensory processing also enables us to subconsciously process sensation that is unchanging so that we can pay attention to new sensation in our environment.

REVIEW OF REGULATION

Efficient sensory processing can contribute to efficient regulation skills. When we understand which sensations are processed more efficiently, we can seek them out to help maintain our nervous system in a regulated state. On the other hand, when we know which sensations are challenging to process, we can prepare for events that contain the more challenging sensations and use strategies to manage the sensations so that we can stay in a regulated state.

We also learn to regulate our nervous systems by learning regulating behaviors from others. Our first relationships are with our parents. We bond with our parents and learn that when we are upset, we are comforted. When we are hungry, we are fed. Our parents co-regulate with us to help us grow and learn how to maintain our own calm alert state. Before we can self-regulate, we learn to co-regulate, match or adjust our level of energy, alertness, and emotion to coordinate with those around us. Adults teach and model self-regulation skills for children so they can learn how to self-regulate. Parents can be excellent role models of self-regulation. You can facilitate co-regulation activities to help students stay calm and focused on the lesson. An example of a self-regulation activity could be 4 square breathing where parents and students slowly breathe in and out as the parent moves their hand along each side of the square.

Many of the techniques we use to calm ourselves and each other are sensory techniques. These techniques can include rocking, singing, hugging, smelling a familiar scent, petting a family pet, or sharing a meal. We can also decrease the sensory input to enable us to self-regulate and can go into a dark, quiet room when we are overwhelmed.

When we are upset or overwhelmed, we may feel scared or frustrated. Our parents comfort us, and we can feel calm, supported and happy again. We learn that emotions are often attached to sensory experiences. The experiences of sensations and emotions become our first memories. We reference our memories throughout our lifetime. They contribute to our understanding of who we are.

REVIEW OF INTEROCEPTION

The interoception system is the sensory system that ties everything together: sensation, emotion, and executive functions. As our nervous system matures, we use our interoception system to automatically scan our body and our emotional state. When we learn to interpret interoception, we know the state of our nervous system and the emotion we are feeling. When we recognize our state, we can choose a strategy to maintain it or change it to return to the 'just right' state; the state of regulation. It is in the "just right" state that sensory processing, emotional processing, and cognitive processing all work together most efficiently. This is the state of learning. It is in this state that we learn about ourselves.

Feelings of competence develop when we know ourselves and what we can do. When we feel competent in our skills, we can develop confidence and take the risks necessary for learning.

When we develop a sense of who we are, we are able to learn that we also belong to our family, our classroom, our faith, and our society. We develop our character, which guides our interactions with the people in our life.

The Sensory Detective Curriculum was written to share information and strategies to encourage the understanding of the underlying neurology of regulation from a sensory perspective. Regulation is possible only when our nervous system is in a calm and alert state. Sensory processing is one of the tools that we can use to support the development of regulation. The development of our character is only possible when the nervous system is regulated.

Stuart Shanker is one of Canada's leading experts on self-regulation. He recognizes that teachers play a very important role in helping students develop self-regulation. (Stuart Shankar, pg. 93). Self-regulation enables many skills according to Dr. Shankar. The ability to self-regulate enables us to recognize which emotions are ours and which belong to another person. The ability to deal with stressors in other dimensions of self-regulation are better in students who can self-regulate.

Some examples:

- *An example of biological regulation:* Amilee feels hungry and wants to go get her snack in her knapsack. She looks at the clock and sees that there are only five minutes remaining until lunch. She decides she can wait.

- *An example of emotional regulation:* Aberdeen says hello to her friend Jayden and Jayden ignores her. Aberdeen felt surprised by Jayden's lack of response. Then she remembered that Jayden had an ear infection and probably didn't hear her. She caught up with Jayden and said hello again in Jayden's field of vision. Jayden smiled and said "Hi, girl!"

- *An example of cognitive regulation:* Mackenzie looked down at his exam. He blanked at question one. "Keep calm," he thought, "what was my clue again? Oh yeah! This answer rhymes with motion … ocean!" He wrote the answer on the exam.

- *An example of social regulation:* Jackson saw his friends at the school fair and began to introduce them to his parents but he could not remember their names. He began by telling a little story about how he and his friends helped the teacher bring the ice down from the staff room and then … pop! … the names were available to him. "Mom and Dad, I'd like to introduce you to Sarah and Cameron, my best friends in school!"

In each of these examples, the regulated state of the student enabled executive functions to be used. Executive functions enable us to fine tune and modify behavior and are dependent on efficient sensory processing and regulation and are necessary for the development of character.

The ability to self-regulate and recognize our own emotions and the emotions of others helps us develop empathy according to Dr. Shankar, and empathy enables us to understand others and can decrease the incidence of bullying.

The ability of a student to regulate his or her own feelings and emotions is a very important life skill. Strong emotions can be disregulating. The negative emotions experienced when a student failed a test can be equally disregulating as the praise another student received from the teacher. Processing strong emotions requires energy. Regulating our emotions is an energy saver—leaving more energy for learning and interacting at school. Social and emotional learning are just as important as teaching reading and writing in school according to Dr. Shankar.

Individuals with self-regulation skills can react to unexpected sensory events throughout their day such as: a light unexpected touch, a forgotten book, or the sound of a fire alarm, but they are able to recover and keep their nervous system in the 'just right' state. Individuals who are more defensive to sensory input react to those same events but are unable to recover and become more disregulated as the day goes on. Sensory events can 'add up' and create explosive behavior that may be difficult to predict.

REVIEW OF EXECUTIVE FUNCTIONS

We rely on our executive functions to successfully go to work and/or school, perform tasks independently, and relate well to others. Executive functions include: inhibition, shift, emotional control, initiation, working memory, planning, organizing materials, and self-monitoring. Efficient sensory processing and regulation are necessary supports to the development and use of executive functions and executive functions are the support to the development of character.

The ability to successfully self-regulate and reliably rely on executive functions can also greatly affect students' character development. It can help motivate them to make positive contributions to their school and community as well as think critically and creatively (www.tdsb.on.ca/elementaryschool/theclassroom/characterdevelopment.aspx).

REVIEW OF REGULATION PROGRAMS

There are many ways that we can work on incorporating self-regulation into the everyday curriculum. There are some wonderful programs to explore:

- *The Alert Program* by Sherry Shellenberger and Mary Sue Williams
  This program uses the analogy that our body runs like a car engine, either "too high", "too low", or in the "just right" speed to help teach self-

regulation to students. Top-down approaches are used, teaching cognitive and language strategies to become aware of the body's state. Bottom-up approaches are also used by introducing various sensory strategies to help change engine speed. They aim to empower individuals to become more aware of their body states and be able to eventually problem-solve independently which sensory strategies they can use to self-regulate.

- *The Incredible 5 Point Scale* by Kari Dunn Buron
  This program was designed to help students with anxiety cope with their stress by systematically organizing social and emotional information. Students sort cards that describe varying situations that they may find stressful into different colored pockets. The pockets are labeled from 1 to 5 to indicate how stressed they think they would feel in that situation. This program offers an anxiety scale, which makes the process of escalation and de-escalation visual, a worry book, and a check in system.

- *The Zones of Regulation* by Leah Kuypers
  This program is a top-down approach and uses cognitive and language strategies to teach self-regulation. Students learn to self-regulate by categorizing the ways they feel into four zones (represented by traffic signs). The program aims to teach students to become more aware of the state of their nervous system and emotions, become better at controlling their emotions and impulses, problem-solve their sensory needs, and help students solve conflicts. This program uses a social thinking curriculum.

- *Stop Now and Plan* by The Child Development Institute in Toronto
  The Stop Now and Plan (SNAP) program was created as a cognitive behavioral strategy and helps teach children to stop before carrying out their automatic response so that they can try to think of a more appropriate way of reacting. The program includes behaviors such as, taking a deep breath or counting to 10. It also includes a cognitive component, such as, thinking of calming thoughts or coping statements such as, "This is hard, but I can do it." It also involves developing a plan for the next steps to take.

Building self-regulation skills and building a community where everyone belongs are keys to successful students. When students feel like they belong they can take responsibility for their space.

Eitan walked through the hallway and saw a discarded water bottle. "That doesn't belong here", he thought, "Someone could slip on it." He picked it up and put it in the recycling container.

Eitan felt a sense of responsibility as he felt this school was his school and he was proud of it. He wanted to take care of it.

EXECUTIVE FUNCTION 2 THE RESCUE

There is a growing awareness about executive functions in our schools and recognition of their importance throughout a student's academic career. Educators Mara Berzins and Nicola Daykin, at the Moncrest School in Toronto, developed a wonderful program to build executive function skills in students called Executive Functions 2 the Rescue. This program introduces students to 10 key executive function skills through characters that represent each skill i.e., Gracie Goal Getter and Suzie Shifter, or 10 EF "superheroes." The program also includes activities to practice, like their "blow off steam" routine. This program strives to develop critical thinking skills through possible scenarios that could happen at school. Berzins and Daykin see the program best used school-wide so that students learn a common language that is consistent among their different classes and grades. This also helps them continue to practice and develop their skills each year at school. For more information, go to: *http://efs2therescue.ca*

General ideas we can incorporate in schools to help build students' overall self-regulation and build a culture of acceptance, belonging and community:

- "Check-in" periodically during learning to see how students are doing and feeling.

- At the end of the day, have students reflect on what was their high point of the day or the low point of their day? What were they most proud of?

- At home, parents can help develop an award wall in front of the spot where their child completes their homework as motivation.

Teaching regulation and executive functions enable us to help students:

- Increase their self-awareness

- Advocate for what they need

CHARACTER DEVELOPMENT FROM A SENSORY PERSPECTIVE

In this final section of the book, we have listed strategies to build the character traits from a sensory, physical, arts, living or classroom space, community space and social point of view, when applicable. There are wonderful ideas from many disciplines listed here (even from the experiences of camp!) but these ideas are by no means exhaustive; they are a starting point. Be sure to be creative! Discussion following the activities can enrich the children's learning. Provide opportunities for reflection and encourage the students to transfer their learning to their day-to-day activities.

Share and discuss stories already in the curriculum and stories from personal experience to broaden understanding.

1. Respect

- We can respect that students with SPD are doing their best everyday

- Even though their behavior can seem difficult, willful or manipulative, we can respect the immense effort students with SPD uses to be in school

- We can give students with SPD choices and respect their choice

- We can respect that the frustration and overwhelmed state of students may be expressed through language, through physiology or through behavior

- Respect the need for movement, stretching and breathing; it can be built right into the daily schedule

- Respect the need for personal space, breaks and modifications to the environment, approach and activities

Physical activities that support understanding and the practice of Respect:

- Yoga—respect the limits of your body and what feels good to you
- Musical chairs—respect the music's direction
- Twister
- Hopscotch—respect where the bean bag lands
- Mother May I?—respect the answer

Arts

- Each student makes a life size outline of themselves and on the torso, they list five things they like about themselves. Then each student lists a characteristic they admire about that person on each outline. Read them out loud.
- Drama scenes (that can be created from the imagination or from actual events)—discuss how the voice volume, choice of words and body language communicated respect and why.
- Ensure books are returned in the right place, scissors are returned blades down, pencils are returned sharpened, etc.

2. Empathy

- The child with SPD cannot be flexible, so we need to be flexible
- We can understand that a student with SPD cannot modulate and modify their responses and they are not consistent in their responses
- We can acknowledge that students with SPD use so much effort, internal resources, strength and coping skills and yet they continue to try

Physical activities that support understanding and the practice of empathy:

- Relay races
- Three-legged race
- Charades—students predict what the actor is experiencing

Arts

- Look at art and guess what the artist was feeling when the picture was created

- Look at dancing and guess what the dancer is expressing

- Mirroring exercise—one student acts out a movement with facial expressions and another mirrors the actions

- Creating cards/banners to celebrate or provide good wishes to students/ staff

Social

- Recall a situation where you needed someone to understand your perspective

3. Responsibility

- We have a responsibility to update the sensory curriculum regularly to accommodate developmental changes, changing interests and age

- We have a responsibility to teach and model organization skills which are essential for school, work, and life

- We have a responsibility to model and teach self-regulation skills

- We have a responsibility to teach executive function skills (problem solving, planning, assessing, foreseeing consequences of behavior, inhibition of responses, controlling impulses, flexible thinking, organization, learning from experience and feelings, time management)

- We have a responsibility to take care of ourselves and each other

- We are responsible to have sensory opportunities built right into classroom duties (movement for delivery, heavy work in carrying books, smells through cooking, tactile needs through art)

- Participation in duties can create a sense of responsibility and a sense of being needed

Arts

- Create a vision for yourself such as a life map, which lists where you are and where you want to go. Have it reflect your interests, goals, and what's important to you

- Group art project with the family

- Play

- Dance

4. Cooperation

- We can work with the student to plan strategies for success in regulation, school function and executive functions

- We can build cooperation with the give and take games and participation in regulation programs

- We can build cooperation by sharing information so that the student knows what is coming up

- We can build cooperation by listening to each other and sharing humor

Physical activities that support understanding and the practice of cooperation:

- Three-legged race

- Egg and spoon race

- Human pyramid

- Broken telephone

- Team sports

Arts

- Group dance

- Group drama presentation

- Building a snow fort

- Tea ceremony

5. Kindness

- We can recognize the effort that goes into trying, noticing and supporting the efforts of others

- We can delay our own gratification to make sure that everyone moves forward

- We can modify our workspace to ensure that sensory needs can be met

- We can modify our approach to match each other's sensory needs

- We can modify schoolwork (allow a student to complete work in parts, work standing up, take tests orally, give extra time)

- We can slow down our interaction with each other to accommodate sensory processing delays, anxiety, and organization difficulties

- We can provide positive feedback to each other

- We can celebrate each other's successes

- We can make sure that everyone feels included, important and part of the group

Physical activities that support understanding and the practice of kindness:

- Mother May I?
- Clapping games
- Skipping games
- Relays
- Three-legged race
- Folk dances
- Native dances

Arts

- Create a kindness catcher role—a student who sees kindness in others and writes/draws it on the board

- Create art to recognize the kindness in ourselves and others
- Which plays/movies show kindness?

Living space

- Caring for a pet
- Caring for a garden
- Creating a kindness jar (acts of kindness are placed within and read at the end of the week)
- Maintaining a bird feeder/water bath

6. Perseverance

- SPD causes function to be inconsistent—keep trying, keep supporting, keep teaching
- Provide regular sensory breaks to regain the calm and alert state in the nervous system to prevent shutting down, meltdowns, running away, over-activity, anxiety, and inattention
- Don't give up in your efforts to interact and support students with SPD; be creative in your strategies until you are successful
- Encourage students to learn from the natural consequences of their actions and understand that mistakes are a natural part of learning

Physical activities that support understanding and the practice of perseverance:

- Long distance running
- Yoga—holding postures
- Learning how to breathe
- Spoon and water relay—filling a bowl across the room one spoonful at a time

Arts

- Long term arts project (knitting, macramé, embroidery, woodworking, sculpture, clay)

- Dance that takes many weeks to learn

- Play that takes many weeks of practice

Living space

- Continuing to tidy (even though it just gets messy again)

- Pen pals where snail mail is used

- Putting away books in the correct place

- Finishing your work—no giving up! Breaks are ok

- Planting a garden

7. Fairness

- Students with SPD have many strengths and interests, find out what they are, label them and use them

- Give students with SPD opportunities to share their strengths—let them teach the unit on dinosaurs

- Set up the classroom environment with sensory needs in mind by modifying the environment to match the sensory needs of the teacher and student (minimize clutter and noise, have a quiet place, give space)

- We all learn in different ways and have different strengths

- A student with SPD may need to use a computer or draw an assignment if writing is challenging

- Offer learning in the sensory modality that is easiest to process for this student

- Modify tasks whenever necessary to build successful experiences

- Give a student with dyspraxia lots of time to organize a response

Arts

- A banner or art project that everyone in the family contributes to
- Folk dancing
- Poetry reading where everyone has a line to read

Classroom space

- Rotating duty roster for classroom duties
- Individualized movement breaks on top of classroom movement breaks if necessary
- Show and tell

Social

- Encouraging students to vocalize what they need to be successful

8. Teamwork

- Identify sensory strengths and challenges and share it with the team (sensory lifestyle)
- Integrate sensory strengths into daily activities with the goal of consistency across settings
- Everyone can support in different ways
- Problem-solve together to discover the underlying reasons for behaviors and strategies to try
- Recognition that we are on the same team and everyone belongs
- When we move forward together, no one gets left behind

Arts

- Collaborative art project
- Producing a play
- Producing an in home choir concert

Living space

- Cooking activities

Community space

- Park clean up
- Going for a Guinness World Record (even if you don't make it!)

Social

- Problem-solving around a problem with schoolwork

9. Integrity

- Practice and model regulation strategies to regain the calm and alert state
- Model what you teach and practice what you preach
- Model empathy and other character traits so that others can learn from you
- Model executive function skills so that others can learn from you
- Interact with students at their level

Arts

- Watching a show and discussing the integrity of the characters
- Draw/write about a time when you have exhibited integrity

Living space

- Items are returned to their correct place
- Schedules warn of any changes to the day

Social

- What would you do if …?—situations are posed to students to see if they can predict what they would do

10. *Honesty*

- Acknowledge our limitations in supporting a student with SPD
- We all need breaks and rest at times—model a choice to take a break
- If something is not working, acknowledge it and create a new strategy to try

Physical activities that support understanding and the practice of honesty:

- Doggie doggie, who has your bone? Who has your iPad?—practice reading faces for honesty
- Mother May I
- What time is it Mr. Wolf?
- Hide and seek—staying in the same spot; not changing
- Dodge ball—acknowledging that you were hit
- Tag—acknowledging that you were touched
- Acknowledging your own needs for help, rest, etc

Arts

- Art—contributing your own work

Classroom space

- Owning up to mistakes and broken items
- Marking your own test

Community space

- Owning up to community partners about mistakes

Social

- Acknowledging mistakes and apologizing
- Providing honest and positive feedback to friends

It definitely takes a village to raise a child (African proverb). Caring for each other, caring for ourselves, and making sure everyone feels included encompasses all of the character traits and ensures that everyone has the opportunity to learn.

Thank you for having fun and learning with *The Sensory Detective Curriculum*. We hope that you have enjoyed learning about sensory processing, the neurology of sensory processing and the assessment of sensory processing.

A society can only move forward at the speed of its most vulnerable individuals. Take care of each other!

RESOURCES TO EXPLORE

Second Step: a program for students from preschool to Grade 8 to help develop social-emotional skills, including empathy, as well as focuses on self-regulation. www.cfchildren.org/second-step/early-learning

Munoz, L.C., Qualter, P., Padgett, G. (2011). Empathy and bullying: Exploring the influence of callous-unemotional traits. *Child Psychiatry and Human Development*, 42, pp. 183–196.

Mahler, K. (2016). *Interoception—the eighth sensory system: Practical solutions for improving self-regulation, self-awareness and social understanding in individuals with Autism Spectrum and related disorders.* Lenaxa. ■

PAULA AQUILLA, B.SC., OT is the author of *Building Bridges through Sensory Integration, 3rd Edition: Therapy for Children with Autism and Other Pervasive Developmental Disorders.* She has worked with adults and children in clinical, educational, home, and community-based settings. She is an active treating therapist who currently runs a private practice serving families with children who have special needs.

SHER ACTIVITIES

Barbara Sher

Here are some activities from my book, *Self-Esteem Games*, that I wanted to share. They may come in handy for you and your family during the quarantine!

ATTITUDE ADJUSTMENTS

Practice putting a positive spin on any situation. As Thomas Edison said, "I have not failed 10,000 times. I have successfully found 10,000 things that did not work!"

DIRECTIONS

Give your child practice in seeing the bright side of life. Take turns imagining positive outcomes to negative experiences. Use the examples below or feel free to make up other scenes.

- **Your friends get invited to a party, but you don't.**

  Possibilities

  1. You end up doing something else you like a whole lot better with someone you love and who really loves you.

  2. You decide that maybe these are not your true friends and you find people who are better friends.

3. You realize that you have been especially negative to your friends and hurting their feelings. Maybe this experience is a "wake-up call" for you to change your behavior.

- **It rains the day you planned to go to the zoo.**

Possibilities

1. You go anyway with a fun pal and a big umbrella.

2. You have the place to yourself and see other animals who enjoy the rain.

3. You end up staying home and playing a dynamite game of *Monopoly*.

4. You put on your slicker and big rain boots, splash in every puddle you find, and look closely at the earthworms.

REPORTER

Get to know each other, while giving the "interviewee" a chance to talk about herself—almost always a welcomed experience.

DIRECTIONS

Sit down with your child in a comfortable place at a quiet time, maybe at the kitchen table after dinner or on the bed at bedtime. Pretend you're a television reporter. Ask as many of these or similar questions as time and the mood allow:

- What is your favorite food? TV show? Game? School subject?

- Where is your favorite place to sit in the house (or in the yard)?

- Where do you like to go in the town?

- What household chore do you prefer or detest.

- What makes you happiest or saddest?

- Which family pet is most like you?

- Which friend would you most confide in?

- Whom do you know that reminds you of you?

- If you could go anywhere in the world, where would it be?

- Do you have a hero or heroine that you admire?

- Would you rather be a rock, tree, flower, or cloud?

VARIATIONS

- For younger children, choose only one or two questions from the list above. Little ones may not be able to answer these questions for them. selves but might easily be able to answer them for their favorite stuffed animal or family pet.

- For larger families, pair players for the interview, then take turns introducing each other with a simple description, e.g., "This is to Joanie and she loves to dance and doesn't mind sweeping. But she'd rather sit beside flowers in her garden."

THE WAYS I AM SMART

Children are smart in different ways. Mathematical and verbal intelligence are measured on IQ tests. Now other aspects of intelligence are being recognized, such as intrapersonal (knowing yourself), interpersonal (understanding others), and kinesthetic (knowing your body).

DIRECTIONS

Ask players to write down the ways in which they are smart or skilled. Family members might want to add to each other's lists.

Examples

1. Mom's List

- I can recognize when I am upset and need some quiet time alone to sort out my thoughts.

- My friends say I am a good listener and like to share their thoughts with me.

- I remember to say nice things to myself when I've just done something stupid. Things like, "Well at least tried!"

2. Kara's List

- I am really good at catching a ball.

- All the kids want me on their team.

- I am a good sport and cheer my friends on.

- I pick up new sports easily,

- I like to read. ■

BARBARA SHER, a *New York Times* bestselling author, believes we each have a genius inside us, our Original Vision, and we've had it since birth. Our culture tends to discourage that vision, but it remains within us, waiting to be fulfilled. She has devoted the last 40 years of her life to saving that Genius, not from its imperfections or a bad self image, but from Isolation and Inner Resistance.

Barbara Sher is a business owner, career counselor, and best-selling author of six books, each of which provides a unique step-by-step method to uncover talent, pinpoint goals, and make dreams come true.

She has been called the "godmother of life coaching" and has presented seminars and workshops around the world to universities, professional organizations, and federal and state government agencies.

PART 5

PRACTICAL MATTERS

FOR AUTISM PARENTS AND ADVOCATES:
13 STEPS TO TAKE WHEN LEADERS FALL SHORT

Ellen Notbohm

A parent's plea I received some years ago wrung my heart. I haven't forgotten his poignant and starkly stated concerns which, in the face of the COVID-19 pandemic and the aftermath that will come when it subsides, are more urgent and pervasive than ever.

He wrote:

I am a single father of a child with multiple neurological and physical challenges. We have so many problems, life-and-death issues. When our leaders and those who make health and education policy are not considering what our children are going through, where will our help come from?

When leaders choose to disregard the needs of our children and the laws protecting them, they choose to disadvantage them, and by doing so, choose to do wrong. It's that simple.

Fortunately, the answer is simple too: our help will come from those who choose to do right. In this lies great strength, because those who want to do right are far greater in number and are present at every level, including leadership positions. Many are in closer proximity to us than the nay-saying leaders.

It was true for me as for most parents, autism advocates and self-advocates, that through my years of raising an autistic child, the higher-ups such as the superintendent of our school district, the state superintendents of public instruction and public health, and the federal Secretaries of Education or Health weren't the ones interacting daily, hourly with my son. His successes came through the efforts of dozens of teachers, doctors, nurses, paraeducators, therapists, administrators, and support staff right down to the school secretaries, bus drivers, medical technicians and receptionists.

These devoted front-liners *chose* to see the potential in my child, *chose* to see value in him, *chose* to challenge themselves to understand, craft strategies, perspectives and paths to learning that brought out the best in him. They had the law behind them, yes, but I saw their work day in and day out. They *chose* to do right by their autistic students and patients (and all children with disabilities) because they wanted to, and they would have even if the law didn't say they had to. And when it was necessary, both they and I challenged the laws, the rules, and the people in charge. I did it with a combination of the support of my son's front-line educators and clinicians, and with reasoned, fact-based demands.

When leaders fail us, our help will come from each other, and from within ourselves. Find your people, your "tribe," and consider taking some of these steps:

1. Stay close. Now more than ever, we are seeing that proximity in the internet age means we can be physically distant but close at the same time we are spreading our wings, our words, our cause and our influence. Proof of the power of this proximity is that the question I'm answering here came to me from the opposite side of the world, an ocean and three continents away.

2. Allow yourself to grieve any hatred, bigotry, and ineptitude going on around us. Let yourself work through the five stages of grief, talk it out with others you trust. You'll be better able to rise to positivity, motivation and resilience if you do.

3. Don't allow yourself to become overwhelmed with the enormity of what we're facing. Whatever the first step is, take it. Then the next, and the next, and the next. Adopt this mantra: increments, not earthquakes.

4. Make yourself visible and heard where perhaps before you weren't. Others have to know we're here before they can help us.

5. Deal always in hard facts. Not assumptions, not guesses, not spin, not falsehood and twisted logic. Knowledge is power. When you have the knowledge, you have the power.

6. Focus on what's doable and winnable. Know your local, state and federal laws so that you don't waste time fighting for something that isn't available or isn't indicated by your child's situation.

7. Recognize when systems or people have set you or your child(ren) up to fail, call it out, seek out others who are being similarly abused, unite, speak out.

8. Do not stoop to the level of leaders or others who engage in name-calling and other detestable speech or images. Never has it been more important to provide our children with consistent modeling of integrity, respect, equanimity and broad perspective.

9. Volunteer. There are numerous ways to make a positive impact for our kids and in your community even if you can't leave your home to do it. Be a grant writer, web designer, editor, proofreader, foreign language translator, online tutor or mentor, online or email buddy for a student, soldier or senior citizen. Offer to record stories or books for emerging, struggling or visually impaired readers.

10. Keep a (respectful) sense of humor. Don't let the baddies rob you of the sanity-saving joy of laughter.

11. Self-care—it's how we stave off burnout. In all you're doing for your child and others, do something for yourself. I like to tell myself to "go outside"—physically, spiritually, artistically, intellectually, socially. "If you

put a small value on yourself, rest assured that the world will not raise your price" (Author unknown). Invest in yourself, the better to reap richer dividends for your own well-being, your child and community.

12. Remember that all leadership is temporary. Leaders leave or topple for many reasons—elections, health reasons, more attractive job offers, threat of exposure of wrongdoing, and the generic "to pursue other opportunities" and "to spend more time with family." Being held accountable is more than some leaders can survive. A leader can't be a leader without followers.

13. And carry with you always the oft-quoted wisdom of anthropologist Margaret Mead:

    Never doubt that a small group of thoughtful committed citizens can change the world. Indeed, it's the only thing that ever has. ■

ELLEN NOTBOHM is the internationally renowned author of the perennially beloved *Ten Things Every Child with Autism Wishes You Knew* and three other award-winning books on autism that have inspired, guided and delighted millions worldwide in more than 20 languages. Learn more on her website at https://ellennotbohm.com.

FINANCIAL PLANNING DURING a CRISIS: AUTISM in LOCKDOWN

Stephen Sicoli

When going through a crisis it can be very hard to focus on the future or even on the current situation.

Although this crisis is difficult, it has brought many people together and has shown the strength of the human condition. You must ensure the safety and security of your family, and this couldn't be truer than with families that have children with Autism.

Although finances can be a touchy subject for many people, it is something that will always play a vital role in our lives so must be discussed regularly as a family. People generally spend more time planning a vacation than planning their futures and lives. The best thing about financial planning? It's NEVER too late to start! It is always good to have financial goals and a road map on how to get there. The hardest step to getting control of your finances is the first one. Once you have a greater understanding of your personal finances, you will feel at ease with the process and will be in a better position for the future. It is important for families with children that have autism to pay close attention to creating a solid financial plan. Any money or assets that a family has now can generate returns long into the future. Even when these families have a plan, it's important to keep it updated because the rules change frequently.

So, how do you ensure lifelong financial security for you, your family and your child?

Here are 5 tips to help you plan ahead despite a crisis.

1. **TAKE A SNAPSHOT.** Find out where you are sitting currently in your finances. Take a good hard look at your Equity. Equity is what you have as assets minus what you have as debt. Next look at Cashflow, what you are spending monthly and what your household brings in. There are many times you have access to funds you didn't realize or may have a higher cash-flow than you thought. If, however, you are finding it hard to make it through to the end of the month or next pay period, it may be time to examine spending habits and possibly cut non-essentials, such as movies or a daily Starbucks. If you do not have a household budget, now would be a significant time to create one; we have already cut down on travel, going out and other things that drain the bank account. Make sure to budget for things like entertainment and eating out if these things are important to you.

2. **DECIDE WHERE YOU WANT TO BE.** Sit down with your entire family to discuss goals and needs. If you want to take a trip to Disney land, great! If it's a new house or a big move to a different country go for it! The main thing is to add it to your plan. Include room for extra expenses as there can often be unforeseen costs with raising a child with special needs. If you plan for the things that are important to you and know what that means, you will have a much easier time getting there. It is important to have long-term goals and several short-term goals that can be easily achieved. You can back-engineer from there and see what your finances will have to be to accommodate your goals.

3. **SPEAK WITH AN ADVISOR.** There are many things that an advisor can do for you; although the most important is to share information. They should teach you what strategies will work best for your situation as there are no cookie cutter solutions for family finances. A few areas to focus on for a family that has children with disabilities would be:

   3.1. Disability Tax Credits & Federal Assistance: Check with your advisor regarding the state or provincial legislation. Your family may be entitled to tax credits, and in some cases, there can be a re-assessment as far back as 10 years. If the bearer of a disability tax credit has no income, a spouse, partner or caregiver may be able to use the tax credit. For American citizens be sure to ask your financial advisor about Social Security Income, Social Security Disability Insurance & how this may affect your ability to contribute to an Individual Retirement Account (IRA). Canadian citizens can acquire a certificate approved by the CRA that allows for tax credits & allowances for caregivers & people who have a prolonged or severe disability. With this certificate you may be eligible to claim the disability tax credit and certain medical & care expenses. If the disability is intellectual in nature, it may also permit you to create a Lifetime Benefit Trust (LBT) which will allow a parent to transfer their RRSP to their child on a tax-deferred basis upon death. This certificate may also give you access to provincial tax credits & benefit programs that will provide allowance and income support.

3.2. Savings Plan: It is never too early to start saving for the future. It is recommended that you put 10% of your monthly income towards savings. The more you can afford to put away, the more prepared you will be when it comes to your children's future. Always look for a tax-advantaged vehicle when investing. In Canada there are Registered Disability Savings Plans (RDSP's) which offer people with disabilities a way to save money in a tax-advantaged account with government contributions. A Tax-Free Savings Account (TFSA) can also be a useful tool when saving. Although there are no government grants, this saving vehicle can be utilized by Canadians with or without disabilities. Be sure to check with your local advisor for solutions that would work for you.

3.3. Education Plan: In Canada there are Registered Education Savings Plans (RESP's) An Investment account in which the government will match a certain percentage of contributions as grants. The parent doesn't initially pay taxes on the money, so they have a double incentive for saving for their children's education.

Taxes are paid when the student withdraws the funds (which will probably be lower than what their parents would have paid on the same money). In the United states there are "529 Plans" that parents can contribute to. Although they do not offer government grant programs, the money contributed to these plans is with after-tax dollars, so they are paid out tax-free. There are also some states that do offer state deductions for parent contributions. Again, I always recommend you speak with your local advisor.

3.4. Plan for a future that may not include you: When any child is under the age of majority, a parent is a legal guardian of the child and is responsible for making decisions on behalf of them. However, when a child becomes an adult that all changes. With families that have children with disabilities it is possible that you may need to continue deciding for your child including finances and personal care decisions. Therefore, it is a good idea to create a sound estate plan for you and your child; in case you are not around or in a position to take care of them. An estate plan could include powers of attorney; which allows you to designate a person to make both property and personal care decisions on your behalf for the child, and creation of a will for both yourself and the child so that any assets can be passed on as you direct.

There are many challenges to estate planning when a child with disability is involved. There must be a plan to provide for the child financially through the course of their lives. It is common practice for these families to set up a trust in their parents will. This type of trust, called a "testamentary trust", takes effect upon the death of the person making it. The parent may choose anyone to act as the trustee, but it should be someone the person trusts to act in the best interests of the child. The trustee will be responsible for managing and distributing those assets in the trust.

Along with the will, it may also be useful for families that have children with disabilities to create a detailed letter of intent. It's not a legal document but can be very helpful to a caregiver or trustee. List any items, like your child's routines, preferences, medicines, and specialists.

Trusts can be quite complicated so if you're thinking about setting up one up you should consult a financial advisor or estate planner who can help you with this task.

3.5. Plan for the worst, hope for the best: There are many situations that can devastate a family, especially ones with special needs. Here are a few scenarios and a few tools that can be implemented to mitigate them:

- Something happens to the primary wage earner: If the primary source of income were to become disabled, get a critical illness, or pass away, how well is your family equipped for that? There are many products in the financial industry that can help cover that, including; Disability Coverage, Life Insurance and Critical Illness Protection. In many cases, there are debts and final expenses that arise upon a loved one passing. Life insurance is in place to take care of this, while also creating an income for the surviving family members.

- Something happens to a non-wage-earning spouse: There are many adverse effects that can happen to a family that are not based in finances. There are many contributions to a household that a non-wage-earning spouse creates and thus a family can have coverage in place to help ease the burden of losing a loved one. This type of life insurance policy can give the wage-earning spouse an opportunity to grieve, take some time off work and spend it with the rest of the family. Of course, money cannot replace a loved one, but it is always better to be in a situation where you do not have to worry about finances while dealing with loss.

- Nothing bad happens: This is what we are all hoping for, although tragedy is so common its almost predictable, it is always good to plan for the best as well. That is why there are insurance policies that include a cash component in which people can access their money tax free and, when set up properly, be used as a retirement fund.

3.6. When speaking with an advisor, make sure you look at your entire family situation and not just the child with disabilities. There are often cases where an advisor can help move things around to free up cash-flow or reduce debt. There are a LOT of different financial tools out there so be sure to speak with a specialist to make sure you are getting the right tools for your particular situation.

4. **FIND A PLAN THAT WORKS FOR YOU.** You work hard for your money, make sure your money works hard for you.

Once you have the proper protections in place for your family, it's time to think about getting the best value from your savings. There are many areas in which you can put your money, from GIC's, bonds and stocks to mutual and segregated funds.

Although the stock market is very tempting, it can be very volatile. Stock trading is best for people who have a good knowledge of investments and the individual companies they are looking to invest in. If you do not have a lot of investment experience, I would recommend putting your funds into a diversified portfolio. This way you can protect your funds on the downsides or any issues in the economy while increasing the potential for growth.

There are a few different kinds of investment funds and depending on your risk tolerance, different ones can be utilized. Mutual funds pool money from the investing public and use that money to buy other securities, usually stocks and bonds. The value of the mutual fund company depends on the performance of the securities it decides to buy. So, when you buy a unit or share of a mutual fund, you are buying the performance of its portfolio or, more precisely, a part of the portfolio's value. Investing in a share of a mutual fund is different from investing in shares of stock. Unlike stock, mutual fund shares do not give its holders any voting rights. A share in a mutual fund represents investments in many different stocks or other securities, instead of just one holding.

Segregated funds are like mutual funds but are sold as an insurance product and therefore have guarantees on the deposited funds. Segregated funds typically have a lower risk investment than a mutual fund, but there are typically guarantees ranging from 75–100% of the funds invested. These can be a great option for anyone risk adverse.

5. **LIVE YOUR PLAN!** This relates back to what I said before about budgeting. If you need to save a bit more money to get the proper savings plan and insurances in place, see what areas you will need to cut back in, and what areas you need to start putting more emphasis on and saving. Always look toward the future; some options may be cheaper but don't provide the proper coverage. Also, not every financial advisor will know about the programs and benefits that can help families with disabilities, so take your time when finding the right one.

It's your choice; you can let this crisis come and go with nothing but a negative impact on your family, or you can start today by taking control of your finances and come out of this crisis better than you went into it. In summary, you need to; take a snapshot, decide where you want to go, speak with an advisor, find a plan that works for you, and LIVE YOUR PLAN! I hope you find this helpful, for more information feel free to send me an email sicoli.stephen@gmail.com. ∎

STEPHEN SICOLI is a licensed associate at one of the largest, fastest-growing financial firms in Canada. Helping Canadian families prepare for their future is only one of the facets of his life. When he is not spending time working with families to achieve financial freedom, he is spending his time out at his farm enjoying nature, working in his garden, and the company of his own family.

SOLUTIONS FOR PARENTS OF KIDS WITH AUTISM DURING LOCKDOWN

Karen Simmons and Ronald Caissie

CHALLENGING ROUTINES

Children on the autism spectrum have a lot of challenges around routines because they are in the habit of going to school and regimented in their routines in their school system. Structure is what they depend on and what helps them make it through the day. When they are thrown off their routines, it turns their entire world upside down causing behavioral meltdowns and anxiety and it takes a long time to get them back on track into their typical routine and balanced. Children with autism can take months to change routines where neurotypicals are much quicker so it's very difficult for children on the autism spectrum to go back and forth from one environment to another compared to a regular household.

It's helpful to bring a child back to a structured routine as quickly as possible through visual tools and social narratives. I know when my son was younger, he could easily understand the written word and could relate to what was happening in the first person. Be sure to provide visual aids and schedules to help them cope and understand with the new routines that will be established. It's important to limit screen time such as television and computer and possibly use sensory tools and toys for entertainment. Transitional periods are very important, so people know what is coming. Social stories can also be a very effective way to help children on the spectrum. A good example would be around social distancing, hand washing and proper use of masks and gloves.

MANAGING FRUSTRATIONS TO AVOID ABUSE

We all have situations that get on our nerves and these times are especially volatile with families in closed boxed in spaces and challenging demands on everyone. Parents are pressured to work and provide a living for their family from home environments while also watching their children on the spectrum and their other siblings. They are also not provided with the tools to help them. We know all too well what can happen when things weren't so challenging. Now during the lockdown and add autism on top of it all, it's the perfect storm for the worst case scenario. Anything can go wrong and often it will if we're not cognisant of the situation, resulting in spousal or child abuse.

In dealing with frustration, we should acknowledge that parents are overwhelmed. They have to take care of their kids all day long, be responsible 24 hours a day and don't get any respite or time away with other people. They're also frustrated and trying to figure out how to do their jobs and take care of the kids. Parents feel that they must be perfect and if they do anything wrong, it could mean the death of one of their disabled children. An example I'd like to give is one of speaking to a father of three children that had autism. He believed that he had to do everything he could to protect them from this crisis, so he isolated himself and his three children. So far, he is 60 days in isolation, working from home and he panics every day and is worried sick. He said he had to be perfect because if he made one mistake as their guardian it could kill one of his children. He clarified that was on his mind, and it was a tremendous responsibility.

When tempers wear down and emotions become fragile, that is a time to watch out. We are all human and therefore it is important to notice signs and learn to calm down. Take five minutes, pay attention to your breath and know that this too shall pass. You must always remember that these are your children and whatever action you do or choose not to do will lay heavy on your mind and your heart. Always remember there are people out there that can help you, such as counsellors, clinical therapists, social workers, and psychologists. These are people you can talk to and are trained professionals often funded by your work programs or your health insurance programs who cover therapists. Please do not suffer alone. There is nothing shameful about talking to someone when you are hurting.

Other helpful strategies to help are breathing exercises, yoga, brisk exercise, taking breaks from watching television and the computer, meditation, eating regularly, sensory tools and engaging in activities.

EFFECTS OF FINANCIAL CONSTRAINTS

Finances are even more difficult than they were before due to these challenging times. It's more difficult to get out to make money as people are being laid off and companies are being shut down. Money is tighter all around as we are all too aware. There are grants and social assistance money available and ways of working online that can be accessed but not everybody can access these, or many people don't know how to access the necessary information. It can be slow, if not impossible, for some people to get money, so it's important to make the dollars stretch. At times like these, families and friends are reaching out to each other like they haven't done for generations.

It's important that you realize that this is not your fault. If you speak to your politicians, they will provide you with the information to guide you to where you can get the money and information you need to survive the crisis. Meanwhile, a financial crisis can lead to stress, anxiety, and depression which can lead to abuse. It is important to talk to a professional and remember there's no shame in talking to somebody outside the family. This could be a professional such as a counsellor, psychologist, social worker, clinical therapist or even your local priest or minister. You'll be surprised how solutions will come about when you open up with others to resolve your situation.

DE-ESCALATING TRIGGERS

Sometimes we get worked up and things get out of hand even in neurotypical relationships, but children with autism can get worked up, and their moods escalate out of control. Here, we need to do everything and anything to calm things down. Calm voices, calm lighting, and look around to see if we can change something in the environment, as our children are very sensitive to touch and sound. Try redirecting the focus of attention and allow more space so behaviors don't get completely out of control. Keep everyone safe as things can escalate quickly.

There are several things parents can do to help themselves de-escalate their children on the spectrum. One is to create a routine for them to get physical exercise by going for walks and playing games with physical activity. This would really help them have something they could rely on and look forward to with anticipation while alleviating a massive amount of stress and anxiety. Advising the child to take a deep breath deep in through their nose into their belly and hold it for ten seconds and breathe out through their mouth. They should do this three times and it should help to calm them down. Another method to help calm them down is to take a shower or a bath, especially in a home environment, however, only in severe situations because when the time comes to go back to school this can't be a strategy. Playing relaxing music and meditative CD's can help calm children and adults down and get them away from the environment.

Again, parents can always speak to professionals online that are trained to discuss these types of situations and advise of supports in your area to de-escalate the child or adult or find out where you should go for help. It's very important that you address issues, so they don't get out of control. There is always someone who is trained to help you do what is best for your situation.

CREATING RESPITE AT HOME

Back in the old days which wasn't that long ago we would take our kids to school and then go to work. The school system managed our children with the support of the para-professionals and educational assistants, so we had a built-in relief system at least during the daytime. What is happening now is that we are with our children 24-7 and have no relief so it's very important that we figure out a way to have respite built into our daily schedules in different ways. The best way to do that is to build in activities that are natural in living our daily lives. Some things that can be considered are sensory kits which include squeeze toys, mats, etc. These are especially good for kids on the autism spectrum because of their issues around sensory conditions and fine motor skills. These types of toys and objects entertain them while providing them with tactile input and help them neurologically. They also distract them from demanding parents' attention and give a sense of relief to the parents. Another way to create respite for parents is for each parent to take turns watching the kids. Maybe the mom wants to take a hot bubble bath with no interruptions. Well, dad could take the kids for a lengthy walk. Or, maybe dad wants to watch a special football game so mom can take the kids on a picnic or something. This way everyone can relax.

Another way you can integrate respite into the home is by teaching life skills in a more involved way. Though it may not seem like respite, it can be a way to provide a structured distraction for the child and give the parents peace of mind that can be built in. This way when the children go back into their schools and communities, they will be more prepared. It is always harder with children on the spectrum to get them to engage in self hygiene, so now is an excellent opportunity to spend more time on it. Focusing on areas such as hand washing, sanitizing, tooth brushing, and so on will help them more in their regular world.

CULTURAL WORK AROUND

It's very important to be cognizant of cultural challenges because they are everywhere with global changes that are going on today. Many children in North America are still taught in the English language by English-speaking teachers and now with the assistants not being part of the equation in some situations it makes it difficult for families to carry on so they just give up. Since we have the internet, it makes it easier to go online and find communities and support groups that have bi-lingual help so that lessons and communication can be translated as long as the parents know to seek this help.

Whether you are translating from Spanish or Mandarin or French, there are groups and online programs that can make it easier to these parents to understand studies and learn how to partially read or write in English. It is also important for everyone to become familiar with the different cultural terminologies, traditions and beliefs. For example, in one culture it is unacceptable to make eye contact with people whereas in another culture it is an insult not to look someone in the eyes.

As far as it goes, in relation to counseling a lot of individuals have issues with cultural concerns. Either they don't understand differences, or they are afraid of differences. They can speak to a counselor, a therapist or a social worker to sort out their feelings and try to come to terms with their emotions. By learning to be accepting of other people's differences and unique ways of being, we all become more humane. You may have a friend or close relative that can speak on your behalf and help to bridge a better understanding for you and your child.

WINNING THE NUTRITION WAR

Kids on the autism spectrum have a lot of challenges around nutrition. Many times, they are sensitive to gluten, casein and soy or other ingredients and they're also very picky eaters. At the best of times they need to have proper nutrition and be challenged by being introduced to trying new foods. In some homes they don't get the proper nutrition and count on the healthy options they have been receiving in school, which have been healthier options. Now with the current crisis this has become a challenge and the children and parents need to be taught proper nutritional information so that the children know what a good meal consists of. Maybe cooking programs that teach the children online about cooking which involve science, math, art, and so forth. The parents could be part of this, which makes a fun time for everyone. Some families are purchasing hydroponic gardening systems in their homes and the entire family takes part in growing their own vegetables. This way they learn all about cultivation, nurturing, gardening, and how to take care of plants. They also appreciate vegetables a lot more when they grow them. We recently watched a series of nutritional webinars hosted by Julie Matthews of Nourishing Hope who presented many top experts presenting evidence-based studies on how certain nutritional strategies help dramatically with autism. She also has a lot of gluten-free, Soy free recipes that make cooking fun for the entire family and gets everybody involved.

In conclusion, these times are certainly the most unusual times we have ever seen and the "perfect storm for the most challenging situation." It is demanding all our energy to come up with solutions for our children. We have worked so long and hard towards inclusion and social acceptance and in what seems to be a heartbeat, it seems to have vanished, but not to worry, the universe is just reinventing itself. A lot of opportunities prevail, and a lot of solutions are on their way to make our world even better than before. We are working to do the same, to help in the best way we know how. By providing the best tools and strategies that we can and use the technology to help as many people as possible on the autism spectrum. ■

KAREN SIMMONS is the founder and CEO of Autism Today, the first online information and resource center for autism worldwide. She brings over twenty years of expertise to the organization and has created over fourteen publications including *Chicken Soup for the Soul, Children with Special Needs*, and gold medal award-winning *The Official Autism 101 Manual*. She has hosted sixty-eight conferences in both the biomedical and behavioral autism and special needs space and is deeply rooted in the autism community worldwide. As a parent of six children, two on the spectrum, she strongly believes in manifesting miracles for the global community in a very big way.

RONALD CAISSIE is a former military officer and parent of a daughter with autism. He formed a disability management company focusing on the effects of trauma on the livelihood of victims and grew it to over 30 offices with his partner. After selling the business he began Ultimate Progress Mediation and Counseling, which focuses on children of all abilities and their families, endeavoring to save his clients time, money, and sanity—helping people come to mutual agreements and leave on a positive note. Ron has a BA, BSW, MEd in counseling and a PhD.

PART 6

SURVIVING AND THRIVING

COOKIES, CATASTROPHES, AND CAR RIDES

Elizabeth King Gerlach

My son's live-in care provider and I brainstormed furiously at the beginning of the COVID-19 outbreak, just as soon as we learned he would probably not have a job for months, and might be limited as to where he could go and who he could see for weeks on end. It's important for most people with autism to have structure and schedules. We thought we could come up with one that would give some reliability and variety to his day. She dutifully wrote his new schedule on the whiteboard in their living room. Within an hour it was all erased, and we were given the very clear message this new schedule would not fly. My son, Nick, is 34, and while he usually depends on the schedule board, he was not having any of this. Not the schedule, not hanging so much with mom, and not the virus either!

During the first few days of the "Stay Home, Stay Safe" order here in Oregon, we witnessed a lot of volatile behavior on his part. By volatile I don't mean physical violence or anything like that, but emotional ups and downs that couldn't be soothed. He threatened to run away and live in the woods, and one day took off for three or four hours without us knowing where he went. The good news was that he remembered to turn on his phone and he remembered to take his hand sanitizer with him. The bad news is we had no idea if he bothered to use the hand sanitizer at the right time before eating a monster cookie he bought from the convenience store, or before washing said cookie down with a red Mountain Dew. (Eating sugar is his way to rebel, and I can relate to this. Maybe you can too?) Despite the threats, Nick came home just before it was getting dark and, after much pleading, lecturing, discussion, etc., he agreed he would not do this again. So far, he's stuck to his word.

Glued to the news apps on my phone, one day I read that in Spain, which suffered horrible fatalities from this virus, the kids could not even leave the house during their lockdown, not even for a walk. *Except kids with autism.* Yes, this exception made total sense. This made me smile inwardly, understanding the tremendous pressure Spanish parents of kids with autism were under, but also knowing that all over the world people who love people with autism needed an extra hall pass of sorts. I could only imagine how hard it was for the families in India, in Afghanistan, and in New York City.

On about the seventh day of our stay at home order, it was obvious Nick was feeling like the world had ended, and he needed to go out, so from that day on, the car ride into the country became our regular coping mechanism of choice. I'm sure the 'ping' on my phone threw the tracking metrics of our entire county lock down compliance numbers off completely. Parents of children with autism often ride our own curves daily, trying to flatten the outbursts, manage the fear, and release the panic. We do what we have to do.

One day out of the blue, my son looked over and said to me, "We're kind of like Noah and the Ark. We've got to stay inside to stay safe." "Yes," I said, very hopeful. (Thank you, God, my son just found his very own window of understanding!) Little miracles like this keep me going. Nick finds a window, a doorway, or some means to make the world make sense to him, and he walks through it to a greater peace.

In the 34 years of raising my son, I find miracles most often come in the form of loving people who help us when we need it. One day Nick was really upset because he couldn't go to the store and get a special garlic bread. Unexpectedly, one of his aides (who hadn't been able to see him due to social distancing) called and volunteered to pick up the bread for him. Another friend of his decided she would call him weekly and teach him how to use FaceTime. She's done this without fail for six weeks even though during the initial run she spent a lot of time talking to his feet as he mastered the geometry of cell phone camera angles.

Sometimes little miracles come in the form of animals or nature. On a particularly bad day the car ride wasn't convincing my son that all was going to be okay. He had been catastrophizing for a good 45 minutes, and I was getting worn out. Then we rounded the bend on a country road and saw a group of horses, and more importantly, a baby foal. No other cars were on the road (remember it's still lockdown) and I stopped the car so we could just sit and stare. The foal walked away, then turned on its new-to-the-earth legs and stared right at us for several minutes. I held my breath, and then next to me heard a big exhale from Nick. The turning point had arrived, the peak in the curve, we'd just made it to the other side. The magic of seeing new life in the form of the foal was a moment of wonder, and that moment made all the difference.

I understand how difficult this world-wide crisis is on my son; it's difficult for me, too. Most of my emotional energy has gone toward helping him get through this pandemic. It's tricky to balance my own emotions when I'm so busy trying to balance another's. Someone I knew died from this virus early on. She was the first recorded death in our county. Her husband is grieving alone without the support of friends and community, and that's heartbreaking. I'm as afraid as anyone else for my life and continually wonder if I'm sanitizing everything correctly and washing my hands thoroughly. I feel grief for the thousands that have succumbed to this illness and gratitude for all the front-line workers who are risking their lives to save people.

This pandemic time will be an "ultimate challenge" as my son likes to say, and none of us will like it much. Every day we are called to do the tasks in front of us. We must remember to be kind to one another and to ourselves every day, every hour, every minute. We must forgive ourselves and others when we lose it. I know we can face this "new normal" with our children and with ourselves because I've been living "just this side of normal" for a very long time. Autism has taught me that love and the forgiveness of meltdowns (and possibly a cookie) are what get us through to the next day, and the next one, and the next. It's this love that creates miracles every day. So, hang in there, you can do this.

Just watch the cookie consumption. ■

 **ELIZABETH KING GERLACH** is the author of *Just This Side of Normal: Glimpses into Life with Autism*; *Apples for Cheyenne: A Story about Autism, Horses and Friendship*, as well as *Autism Treatment Guide*.

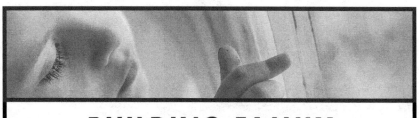

BUILDING FAMILY RESILIENCY

Hartley Steiner

The world has turned our routines upside down, and life has gotten a lot harder for most of us. Working from home, managing kids, and school—without the teams of people we have relied on (therapists, aides, teachers) is daunting and overwhelming. It is as if all of our well-laid plans and structures were somehow swept out to sea, leaving us behind on the shore to pick up the pieces. I know that this wasn't what you expected, and how overwhelming it is to be thrown into this whirlwind with your family. And I am sorry you're going through this. But I am also hopeful that this experience will provide us with some positives—a silver lining or two—that continues to tell us that difficult times have meaning and there is resiliency to gain.

I, too, have been thrown into working from home while managing my three sons' schooling—all of my sons normally have teams of professionals at school that I rely on—and I am missing the support and frankly the break of having them all at school where I am not the one in charge. We have shifted to distance learning, and distance therapies—OT, SLP, psychologist and psychiatrist appointments all on Zoom—and I am thankful for the connection, but still am painfully aware that some days it doesn't feel like enough. I am at times somehow proverbially underwater, wishing I had my routines and structure back. But my secret weapon is resiliency. I have a resiliency plan that I lean on which allows me to maintain my mindset of empowerment and gives me a positive outlook on dealing with crisis. I have survived worse, and I know I can survive this. And even better, my boys and I can thrive through it because our family is resilient. And yours can be too.

Maybe you haven't thought a lot about the value of resiliency, or maybe you have. I am here to tell you that taking an active approach to increasing personal and family resiliency offers each of us the power to pull ourselves up from underwater, or better yet, not get swept out to sea at all.

WHAT IS RESILIENCY?

Resiliency is defined as *"the ability to recover quickly from difficulties."*

Being resilient—and having a resiliency plan in place—gives us the power to take hold of a crisis when it begins and move through it with minimal adverse effect. The mindset that we can and will not only be able to meet the challenge, but we have the resources to do so is key.

As we all know stress isn't good on us; mentally, physically or emotionally. Living with chronic stress during a crisis—where the "threat" never ceases, and we are constantly triaging from a place of already depleted energy—isn't sustainable. This is why building family resiliency is so important to our own personal health, and the health of our family unit. In order to be prepared, to have something to draw upon during unexpected (or sometimes expected) times of crisis is how you build resiliency. We must intentionally develop the skills necessary to triage emergency, then refill our reserves. In short, we must prepare for the unexpected.

THE BASICS OF RESILIENCY.

The basics of resiliency are self-care, communication and mindset. These three, along with a range of other supports, give us our ability to prepare for the unexpected.

SELF-CARE. Self-care is what you need to refill your energy mentally, emotionally, physically and spiritually. During times of great stress, or crisis, it is important that you are taking care of your needs and safeguarding your energy, so you have it in reserve for dealing with all that comes at you. Think about what you need to refuel yourself. Good sleep, time to work, some peace and quiet, nature, a pleasant walk. What kinds of things can you do to make sure you are recharging? Think of it as a realistic list, be practical. Now think about what the other members of your house need. Do your kids need one-on-one time? Do they need to walk, or get away from their siblings? What about your spouse or partner? Ask the members of your family what they need to make each day *easier* on them? The goal during times of chronic stress is to elevate it or minimize it, not to be super productive. I know the idea of self-care can be daunting, if not impossible, especially when you have high needs children, but it is imperative that you lower your stress. This isn't a luxury; this is a necessity. Now that you are thinking of the things you need and your family needs for life to be *easier*, that brings us to communication.

COMMUNICATION. This is the step where the adults, and children if they are old enough and able to be included, sit down and talk about what each individual needs and how to get it. Don't over-complicate it. Identify support systems that you can access remotely for now, or in person later. Can you buy yourself an hour while your child watches a movie? Can you skip cooking and dishes and have cereal? Can you ask a friend or family member to have a zoom call? Can you face-time with a therapist? Get creative and work together to find solutions that allow each member of the family to recharge, refuel and regroup daily.

Talking about the impacts of stress on everyone is a step towards stress relief in and of itself. It is ok to admit this is hard, and that we all need help. Opening up the discussion for your kids allows them a safe space to talk about how they are handling it and gives them permission to acknowledge the difficulties they may be having. This conversation is a good time to remind your kids (and yourself) that they are not alone, and that you are a team.

MINDSET. This is where we focus on the silver linings. I know how hard it is to be positive about things when you are in crisis—or in our collective case a global pandemic—but what you focus on is what you will grow. Shifting into a positive mindset, or continuing it is often centered around gratitude. Being thankful for what is good, what is going well, is a key part to our mental health.

I use this strategy at home with my sons, to make sure we don't get stuck in the complaining mode about everything we can't do. I listen to their concerns, but get them focused on what they are gaining—so much down time to regroup, nothing is over scheduled, they have more time together, time to learn new things, or just endless hours chatting on discord while playing video games—they are a part of history in the making. And I remind them I know for sure that *this too shall pass.*

Now that we have gone over the basics of resiliency, you can make a plan. Having a plan in place is what you lean on when a crisis comes up. It is a physical reminder that you have done this before and survived, and you can do it again, only better. When a crisis comes up, small or large, something you've dealt with before or not, you can walk through the plan for stress management: self-care (making things easier), communication (what needs to be done and who/how it will be done) and mindset (being grateful for what you have and knowing you can and will make it through). Setting this simple strategy in motion feels empowering. And regaining that control helps to move you from being swept out to sea to steering the ship.

RESILIENCY IS A PRACTICED SKILL

Let me say that again: Resiliency is a practiced skill. This is something you learn and build on. Much like learning to play piano, or implementing a sensory diet at home, it is something that at first may seem daunting, or confusing as to how you'll ever get it in place, but over time you will build it. Your resiliency plan will get broader, and your ability to triage problems will become faster and have a lighter impact on you and your family. Add the structure of a resiliency plan to life at your own pace, work at it, regroup and try again.

And be gentle with yourself. ■

HARTLEY STEINER lives in the Seattle area with her three sons. She is the award-winning author of the SPD Children's book *This is Gabriel Making Sense of School, Sensational Journeys*, and *It's Just a What?* She is a life and parenting coach, working with individuals and groups, as well as an active advocate and speaker. She has contributed to *S.I. Focus Magazine* and *Autism Spectrum Quarterly*, among dozens of other websites and blogs. You can connect with her online at HartleySteiner.com and on all social media platforms @HartleySteiner.

ATTITUDE of GRATITUDE for AUTISM

Karen Simmons

know it can be especially hard in times like these to feel grateful for anything, especially with behaviors raging, routines out of whack and parents in turmoil not knowing what to do.

However, when things go right, when people connect, laugh, and share the wonderful things that are going on, it makes us all feel better and after all that's really ALL we are is FEELINGS.

We were moving out of my house after exactly 30 years and my son with autism, Jonny, unplugged the internet by mistake, had to stop the entire moving process at midnight, evaluate the entire situation, and research how to reset it right. It turned out that literally all he really had to do was to plug it in again! We all laughed. He had his moment in the sun.

Here are some very special words shared with me by my dear friend Dr. Jerry Jampolsky, founder of The Centre of Attitudinal Healing, specializing in catastrophic illness when I told him about the coincidental occurrences in my life.

"Karen, coincidences are God's way of remaining anonymous".

At the age of 95, Jerry now says the following!

"Fear can be the most virulent and damaging virus known to humankind."

— Gerald Jampolsky, MD

This has pointed me along a pathway towards many magical moments over the past 25 years, especially around Autism Today, *Little Rainman, Chicken Soup,* and the work that I completed when I became an Attitudinal Healing Training Facilitator in 1997.

The Attitudinal Healing Centers work around traumatic situations, prisoners, children's death and dying and what people have the hardest times going through. With COVID-19 in the world, it is the perfect time for his work.

I would like to invite you to read through these twelve principles of Attitudinal Healing. If you embrace any (or all of) the concepts, they may help you during this tough time. If not, that's fine too.

Attitudinal Healing is based of the belief that it is possible to choose peace rather than conflict, and love rather than fear. It is love that is the most important healing force in the world and we need this now more than ever.

Each principle is in **bold**, and my comments follow.

THE TWELVE PRINCIPLES OF ATTITUDINAL HEALING ARE:

1. **The Essence of Our Being Is Love**

    At the core of everyone there is good ... that spark that started at the beginning of life.

2. **Health Is Inner Peace, Healing Is Letting Go of Fear**

    Fear stifles our creativity and choosing to embrace our internal peace distracts any perceived fear, which is merely an illusion.

3. **Giving and Receiving Are the Same**

    As we inhale, we also exhale. If we learn to accept from others and give from our hearts, we will feel the same reciprocal energy flow through ourselves.

4. **We Can Let Go of The Past and Of the Future**

    Living in the now is all there ever really is. The past is gone, and the future hasn't happened—nor does it usually happen in the way as we project.

5. **Now Is the Only Time There Is and Each Instant Is for Giving**

   Letting go helps us recognize the synchronicity in the universe.

6. **We Can Learn to Love Ourselves and Others by Forgiving Rather Than Judging**

   When we love and forgive everyone in our own hearts, this frees us. Judgment of others assumes a power position rather than a position of love.

7. **We Can Become Love Finders Rather Than Fault Finders**

   What we focus on expands. Seeking love, we find more love and if we are looking for faults, we find more faults.

8. **We Can Choose and Direct Ourselves to Be Peaceful Inside Regardless of What Is Happening Outside**

   We are in control of our feelings and our thoughts. What we focus on fills our hearts.

9. **We Are Students and Teachers to Each Other**

   The more we know, the more we realize there is to know, and we are always learning and teaching. In teaching, we also continue to learn.

10. **We Can Focus on The Whole of Life Rather Than the Fragments**

    Keep in mind the big picture, "this too shall pass" helps. Minor things are small. Let them go.

11. **Since Love Is Eternal, Death Need Not Be Viewed as Fearful**

    We are forever who we are. Our bodies are carriers of our entities. What makes us *us*, feelings, emotions, happiness, and sadness are not physical.

12. **We Can Always Perceive Others as Either Loving or Fearful and Extend A Call of Help for Love**

    Everyone ultimately wants to be loved and accepted for who they are—regardless of abilities, race, sex, religion or any other perceived difference.

Lovingly,

Karen Simmons, Founder of Autism Today ■

P.S. We are here to help if you need us. Love is constructive, and fear is a VIRUS

 **KAREN SIMMONS** is the Founder and CEO of Autism Today, the first online information and resource center for autism worldwide. She brings over twenty years of expertise to the organization and has created over fourteen publications including *Chicken Soup for the Soul, Children with Special Needs* and gold medal award-winning *The Official Autism 101 Manual*. She has hosted sixty-eight conferences in both the biomedical and behavioral autism and special needs space and is deeply rooted in the autism community worldwide. As a parent of six children, two on the spectrum, she strongly believes in manifesting miracles for the global community in a very big way..

THRIVING ON A THEME

Julie Clark

hange is rarely welcome for many of us. Not knowing what will happen in a few days, let alone a few weeks, ups stress levels, too. The COVID-19 pandemic has us considering all sorts of things. And this should include taking care of ourselves, too.

For our family Kristina, our Aspie, is older now, off to law school. Like most in school, she's taking classes virtually and must shelter in place. She currently lives in an apartment off campus and hasn't been able to leave it in a very long time. Due to being in the higher risk category, she gets groceries delivered and hasn't been able to walk around town in weeks. Anxiety has reared its head more than once and she does work hard to combat it. In true form, she's making the most of the things, finding that drawing upon old loves helps pass the time and move her thoughts to a better place. Even though coursework keeps her busy, she still has down time.

As for my husband and I, we also work to find structure, plus healthy diversions, during this time, too.

The following suggestion is all Kristina's; she's given me her blessing to share it with you. To break the monotony of being cooped up for so long, she decided to create a Disney Makeup Challenge. Disney truly is an old love; she's been a Disney fan as long as we can remember. Her love of Lilo and Stitch has expanded to other stories, countless characters, and magical memories made in Disneyland and Disney World that she goes back to time and again. What's her idea, you ask? Ah, right! Every day for an entire month she comes up with a specific Disney theme, then chooses makeup to match. This meant green eye-shadow for Tiana's day, and apple red lipstick for Snow White's. She also added a touch of artwork when it was Sally of *The Nightmare Before Christmas* fame's turn. But she doesn't stop there; she coordinates her clothing, too. It's been so much fun to see what she'll come up with each day!

Even though you may have zero interest in makeup or fashion, you could apply this thought in other ways. You could choose to dress up in the colors your favorite character is known for. Or you could go all out and dress as them for the day. You could change characters each day, too. You could even draw them, instead.

Not into movies or books? You can create your own theme to pass the time (as well as add a bit of structure to it). There really are no rules to this except to have fun!

We love our daughter's idea because it takes time to execute. It takes time to come up with the day's palette, put it all together, then snap a pic to Insta-gram for a group of family and friends to see. It truly adds a smile and a bit of lightness to everyone's day—including hers! It engages the concept of self-care, too. Self-care is so important for all of us, especially when life takes turns we'd rather it not.

Another thing this Disney Makeup Challenge does is take our minds off the current situation. In short, it gives all of us something positive to look for-ward to. We look forward to seeing her interpretation of today's character or movie, and she looks forward to planning it all out, pulling out the brushes and pallets, creating a temporary masterpiece.

That's another thing, too. It's so very important we are aware of what is going on around us in relation to the coronavirus. We must take responsi-bility to understand what the regulations are in times like these and abide by them. But we also need to make sure they don't become another interest, so to speak. It is wise and good to limit exposure to news on the virus; being aware of what we need to be, then letting the rest go. Even though we may never catch COVID-19, listening to the pundits, the statisticians, the commentators ad nau-seam can affect our psychological well-being. Be kind to yourself—and those you share your home with—and limit your intake of this information only to what is necessary.

This brings up another thought. When talking with a colleague of mine recently, she reminded me that therapy is still an option for many of us, even with social distancing in effect. If fact, Kristina still connects with her therapist, and they do so virtually. Is it ideal? No. Is it beneficial and effective? Yes!

One side note: Keep in mind when you are having virtual consultations to choose a location where you have the best chance of privacy. Sitting on the porch may seem private, but our voices can carry on the wind. One trick Kristina's childhood therapist used was to play music in the waiting room. This lessened the chance those waiting would overhear the conversation. Perhaps you might wish to try the same?

The pandemic situation is tough for us all. It is imperative we find ways to navigate it the best we can; creating structure and new routines can be a part of that. Take time for self-care, take time for mental health breaks, and, most of all, take time to remember what gives you joy every day. For Kristina, deep dives into the world of Disney is a salve. For my husband, it is a jigsaw puzzle or taking our overgrown Yorkie for a walk. For me, it's rediscovering the joy of reading fantastical stories, set in a time that doesn't resemble this one in the slightest, or standing outside, under an oak tree, imagining the earth taking all the stress away then replenishing me with something better.

We will get through this. Let's be sure to take care of ourselves along the way so we will come out strong on the other side! Use this time to rediscover what makes you happy. You just may find it is a key that will help move your mind into a better place. ∎

JULIE CLARK is a mother of a daughter with Asperger's Syndrome, who possesses a strong desire to increase awareness and understanding of the "pink" in the autism spectrum. Julie holds a Bachelor of Arts degree in Communications, with minor studies in French and Studio Art. She is author of *Asperger's in Pink: Pearls of Wisdom from Inside the Bubble of Raising a Child with Asperger's*.

THE PALMERS ARE FLOURISHING IN THE NEW NORMAL

Melissa Palmer, MD

The new normal for the rest of the world is not at all new to us. With two daughters diagnosed with Autism/Anxiety/ADD and two parents who probably would have benefited with diagnoses of their own, the Palmer family has been business as usual during a time that has been markedly horrendous for millions around the world. How is this so? Are we callous, unfeeling monsters with no regard to others' feelings? Not really. It's quite the opposite.

As my 14-year-old tells me often, "We can't turn off our brains." In the old days, back before quarantine, we lived in a world of backyard bashes, staff meetings, town events, crowded shopping malls, and churches brimming with shoulder to shoulder people. These are the things that make me shudder, yet I hear people lamenting they miss them the most. They yearn for the bright lights, the hustle and the bustle of small talk in the store, loud busy restaurants, or waiting in line at the movie theaters. I don't fault these people for feeling, but these are the type of things that have brought nothing but anxiety, terror, and heartache to our family's everyday lives. Now they've all gone poof, and for us, it's not so bad.

For years I have tried to explain why we never attend get togethers or why we don't go to restaurants unless it is during off-peak hours. When I am in the office at work, I sit on the floor with everything I need to look at spread out so I can make it make sense. I also work in the dark. My co-workers have gotten used to me squatting on the floor, but at least a dozen times a day I shrug in-quiring minds off with a nod as if I'd forgotten to turn the light on. At home I can sit as I am now, in a dark room, listening to "Relaxing Music for the Dog" on YouTube, because in this new normal Hopper can lay his head on my foot as I work, something I never realized does more for my racing brain than any pill, panacea, or meditative chant. My husband can work as he loves to work: as he is now with four different audio sources playing in the background because it helps him focus. (Could you imagine doing this in a "normal" office?)

Hello. We are the Palmers. The world before quarantine is a place we have all individually struggled to fit. Between our two daughters we have had ONE traditional birthday party in the span of 14 years. We don't go to malls and hate dinner parties. If you ask us over for a holiday, we are going to say no. If we win an award, it would be best to send it in the mail. The most uncomfortable place I've ever seen my husband is around other people. I wash my hands every time I touch something and that's before Dr. Fauci told me to do it. We are a sensory sensitive bunch who for the first time in the longest time I can remember are all happy. Since quarantine began, we joked that we may have been training for this moment for our entire lives.

Sophie, 14, has struggled with school for her academic career, not so much for the academics but the combination of stimulation and "peopling" has prov-en for her to be agony. Sophie is taking an inventory of every sound, smell, sight, and sensation around her, while a running commentary of every threat, conta-gion, pathogen, poison, or cataclysmic, atmospheric, or apocalyptic event runs concurrently like a soundtrack in her mind. The reality of everything around her and the possibilities of what is coming compound with the irreversible damages already done in the past twist inside her inner thoughts like a tornado. ALL. DAY. LONG. Try getting through a day in an average 8th grade class like that. The simple sound of another student's pen scratching the paper next to her bores into her head in a "normal" classroom, and her way of coping is to tap, hum, bang her desk or (much to the chagrin of her teachers) talk about some-thing that makes her comfortable—at length. You can see where this could be frowned upon in a standard classroom setting.

At home, she is the master of her own sensory surroundings. She sits (like her mom) in a room with no lights on, hovered gargoyle-like over whatever she's working on, sometimes on the floor or on the edge of the bed. She scribbles away on notes and problems like a mad scientist and finishes a day of schoolwork in the course of 40 minutes. Sophie is a purpose driven and at home she can attack that purpose until she is through with no worries about timers, school bells, announcements, or watchful eyes.

Now she has the freedom to balance her energy with her time, and much more efficiently. Anxiety is the great time sucker, evidently, because tasks that would normally take two days at school are things she can dispatch within minutes. Undistracted sensory focus is an amazing thing! With the rest of her day she buries herself in the things that make her the most comfortable: creating music, short films, and digital realms that would humble the most impressive city planners or architects. Since March, she's produced to movies, and has written not just a song but an album, recording all the instruments and laying them down as tracks. We have seen creativity pour from this child like a fountain. Not to mention the most incredible side effect of quarantine yet. For the first time in a very long time Sophie is sleeping at night!

Note: I cannot remember this happening. *Ever.*

Lily, 11, is our self-proclaimed introverted potato. For our 5th grader, it wasn't the academics of the regular school day, but the "peopling" that was the hardest. Pre-quarantine Lily would beg in the mornings crying for me not to send her to school. These were not phony tears either. The days of the world that people lament missing were, for our family, filled with emotionally wrenching goodbyes, screaming, begging, and leaving her at school holding back my own tears from the guilt. Lily hates the feeling of looking at people or people looking at her, and in elementary school that is a hard feeling to avoid. Her answer is usually retreating to a world where no one can reach her, going quiet for hours at a time, focusing on drawing, doodling or coloring lines. In the "normal" school setting, those kinds of breaks are near impossible and normally incur censure. (Drawing in textbooks is rightfully frowned upon!) Something as simple as lunch in the regular school setting was Lily's most hated period in the day. A brightly lit cafeteria filled with chatter, crinkling papers, and the smells of other kids' lunches spun her into panic attacks and crying fits. Most kids love gym and recess. For Lily, these required Herculean attempts to keep her heart from racing. The effort to self-regulate in a regular school day was exhausting, so much so her muscle control usually failed in the afternoon. When she was younger she would fall out of desks or drop things, bringing unwanted attention to a child who much would prefer being invisible on any given day. In the days most people miss, Lily would come home with a headache and an emotional meltdown that would span an hour a day and lay in her bed until almost dinner before becoming herself again. For Lily, the effort to appear "normal" during a school day took so much effort on her part that when she came back home, she would collapse in a heap.

But now we're on Palmer scheduling. If it takes 47 minutes to eat one pancake, that's how long it takes. If it is too loud in the kitchen, Lily can work in the playroom. In this new world, Lily is not riddled with worry about what other kids will say to her. She is allowed to wear the one outfit that doesn't "feel scratchy" for three days straight without a peep from her schoolmates. If she stutters, misspeaks, or mixes up words, no one here will point it out, snicker or giggle. She is not self-consciousness about the way she speaks or reads out loud. In short, she's not overwhelmed, and now that that's lifted something unbelievable has happened. The "introverted potato" speaks more in Zoom meetings with her classmates and teachers than she's ever spoken before. She's having virtual "playdates" with friends, inviting classmates to watch her draw and play *Minecraft*. For the first time (ever) Lily is inviting other people into her world. From the comfort of her room and through the lens of her tablet, she contributes to class discussions, shows off her drawings, and Pokemon collection. She's even brought her cats and her bearded dragon to class.

From the safety of quarantine, Lily has come out of her shell.

We have our moments like everyone else in this "new normal," where frustration kicks in and we're bickering over who ate the last Marshmallow Peep. That's the reality of four people living in a house with two big dogs, three cats and a bearded dragon. It can become a challenge for most, but for us this way has always been the normal. The newness for us is for the first time we are all truly comfortable. We are quarantined (as we've always lived) with three other people who understand our sensory needs and we are all incredibly aware of our family members' strengths and pitfalls. We rely on, inspire, and challenge each other to make the best of this time while it lasts, because for us, it's not that bad. When you have four people working for and with each other and then cut out the anxieties of the external world that mostly terrifies all of us— We Palmers Are Flourishing!

Note: In the world Pre-Quarantine I'd never get to write this. ■

 **MELISSA PALMER**, author of *Baking for Dave*, is a writer, nerd, baker, part-time kitchen dancer, wife, and full-time mom. She pulls from her experiences with her own daughters—the two superheroes who shape and guide her life—to create the world and characters seen in *Baking for Dave*. When she's not writing, she's biking or running (either on the road or after one of the many animals in her menagerie).